DATE DUE

THE
Bertrand Russell
CASE

A Da Capo Press Reprint Series

CIVIL LIBERTIES IN AMERICAN HISTORY

GENERAL EDITOR: LEONARD W. LEVY
Claremont Graduate School

THE
Bertrand Russell
CASE

*Edited by John Dewey
and Horace M. Kallen*

DA CAPO PRESS • NEW YORK • 1972

Library of Congress Cataloging in Publication Data

Dewey, John, 1859-1952, ed .
    The Bertrand Russell case.
    (Civil liberties in American history)
    CONTENTS: Introduction, by J. Dewey.—Foreword, by A. C.
Barnes.—Behind the Bertrand Russell case, by H. M. Kallen.
[Etc.]
    1. Russell, Bertrand Russell, 3d earl, 1872-1970. I. Kallen,
Horace Meyer, 1882-   joint ed. II. Title. III. Series.
KF228.R8D4   1972   344'.73'078   78-37289
ISBN 0-306-70426-9

This Da Capo Press edition of *The Bertrand Russell Case*
is an unabridged republication of the first edition
published in New York in 1941. It is reprinted by
special arrangement with The Viking Press, Inc.

Published by Da Capo Press, Inc.
A Subsidiary of Plenum Publishing Corporation
227 West 17th St., New York, New York 10011

Manufactured in the United States of America

The Bertrand Russell Case

THE
Bertrand Russell
CASE

*Edited by John Dewey
and Horace M. Kallen*

NEW YORK

The Viking Press

1941

CONTENTS

[5]

[6]

Introduction

It is fitting to say a few words about the origin of this book. When it became apparent that the forces of reaction, bigotry, and political cowardice were powerful enough to obstruct the cause of fair play and of intellectual freedom in the case of Bertrand Russell's appointment to a chair of philosophy in the College of the City of New York, Dr. Albert C. Barnes engaged him for a period of years at the Barnes Foundation, Merion, Pennsylvania. Russell's lectureship is now progressing successfully and to the satisfaction of all concerned. No one, Justice McGeehan to the contrary notwithstanding, has been instigated to commit any "damnable felony." It may, indeed, be doubted whether the Justice really believed anything of the kind would happen if Mr. Russell were appointed to a chair in City College.

But Dr. Barnes was not satisfied with this action in behalf of religious toleration and intellectual freedom. He felt that the social importance of the case demanded there be a public record of the issues involved. This book is a result of his suggestion. Fairness to him and to the writers of the essays makes it advisable to say that the authors of the essays were selected not by him but by a group representing the Committee for Cultural Freedom, one of the first organizations to take an active part in condemnation of the attack on education and culture involved in the Russell case. Nor did

Dr. Barnes make any suggestions, much less give any advice or instruction, as to what contributors could or should say.

The various contributors represent different philosophical and social standpoints. They are agreed upon one point: the unqualified necessity of honest discussion by competent persons, using the method of intelligence, the scientific method. For they know the alternative is some aspect and degree of totalitarianism. It is probably true that because the war waged by totalitarian powers came at a time when it distracted attention from the Russell case it became easier for the cohorts of darkness to "get away" with their campaign against the democratic method of discussion. But it would be a bitter irony if protest against totalitarianism abroad should be a factor in fostering recourse to totalitarian methods in this country.

The writers are also agreed that the social importance of the present case far transcends the injustice done to Mr. Russell personally, great as that is; and that it also transcends the question of the merits or demerits of the particular views he set forth. The reasons for this belief are given in the essays that follow. The Mayor, who has to accept a share in the responsibility for allowing an attack upon moral and intellectual freedom to go by default, had occasion later to protest when the Justice, who appropriated for himself the duty of appointment belonging to a duly constituted public agency, did the same sort of thing in the case of a public commission having authority in the matter of public transit. In the latter case, the act of the Justice was found to approach usurpation. There are those who believe that public access to the sources of knowledge and light are as important as means of access to rapid transit. But this aspect of the action of the Justice, who stood steadily in the way of permitting an appeal to a higher court and in

[8]

the way of allowing Mr. Russell to exercise the supposedly elementary right of self-defense, is but the technical manifestation of an underlying attempt to apply the lynch law of popular outcry to settle an issue where the enlightened judgment of competent educators who have no political or theological ax to grind was on the other side.

Legally speaking, the particular case with which this volume deals is now a closed issue. But the issue underlying it is no more settled than the Dred Scott case settled the slavery issue. There are events which do more than tell in what direction the wind is blowing at a given time. They have a pivotal, a crucial, importance. They may become precedents for later activities in the same direction. Then a change of angle that subtends a small arc at the outset comes in time to include a vast space. Or the same event may arouse protest; it may stir forces that had been lulled into apathy. So far as public institutions of higher education are concerned, and so far as the whole cause of unfettered public discussion of social and moral issues is at stake, it may well turn out that the Russell case is an event of this pivotal kind. The turgid rhetoric and the dishonest abuse engaged in during the process of winning a temporary legal victory for reaction and intolerance may possibly contribute to creation of a long black period in our intellectual life. But the extreme this reaction went to in flouting of fair play and of freedom may, on the other hand, help clear the atmosphere of foul vapors and so assist the light of intelligence to shine more brightly.

Belief in the social importance of public discussion of moral problems, when it is conducted upon the plane of scientific method and with a sense of public responsibility, is, as I have said, the bond which unites those who have written this book. The belief is accompanied by the hope that

[9]

this book may contribute in the same degree to the happier conclusion of the two possible ultimate results for the freedom of the human spirit and the democratic way of life.

JOHN DEWEY

Foreword

This volume is neither an attempt to build up a vindication of Bertrand Russell in the matter of his ousting from the faculty of the College of the City of New York, nor a presentation of arguments in favor of academic freedom. The book is simply the record of an inquiry into the *facts* of the case—an inquiry conducted by specialists qualified to examine its manifold aspects and to relate their findings to the principles of justice, law, humanity, and common decency, as these are set forth in the Constitution of the United States and in the Bill of Rights.

It is Democracy that needs to be vindicated, not Bertrand Russell. From the time of the initial charges against Russell until the enforcement of the court decision that wantonly injured him, neither Democracy nor Russell was given an opportunity to raise a voice in their defense. This attempt at character-assassination is a black mark on America's escutcheon, in some respects even deeper in tone than was the bodily assassination of Sacco and Vanzetti; deeper because the Italians were accorded the formality of trial in a court of justice and Russell was not. The two cases are paralleled by the facts in common that no proof of the charges can be established and that condemnation was inspired and fostered by the conjoined efforts of bigoted authoritarians holding positions of power. The court decision in each case has been proved to be a parody of wisdom, justice, and public welfare.

[11]

Not any of the essays in this volume can be intelligently classified as a cry over spilt milk; more accurately can they be termed a united effort to construct a container that will be proof against future similar spillings. No well-informed person would question the competency of each of the contributors to do a good job; their tools, material, and workmanship are offered here for inspection.

The problem is only incidentally concerned with education in schools, colleges, and universities, and it is a mere coincidence that a particular individual is involved: its field encompasses the whole of American life in that it affects the most cherished right of every person, whatsoever be his work, social rank, religious creed, or his political beliefs. In a word, the stake is the lifeblood of Democracy, the right of every individual to be free from the tyrannical acts of dictators which, as in the Russell case, usurp the rights of the people, violate the basic principles of the American Constitution, hamstring education, and bring disgrace upon the whole nation.

ALBERT C. BARNES

BEHIND THE
BERTRAND RUSSELL
CASE

By Horace M. Kallen

Behind the
Bertrand Russell Case[1]

I

THE Bertrand Russell case presents a challenge to American intellectual life and American education to which, the *New York Herald Tribune* declares, "no friend of civil liberty and academic freedom can remain indifferent."

The case grew out of a churchman's assault upon Bertrand Russell's person and principles after he was appointed to teach mathematics and philosophy in the College of the City of New York.

The appointment had been made on the basis of the appointee's record and reputation. He was, at the time, teaching philosophy at the University of California at Los Angeles, and designated to give the William James lectures at Harvard in the fall of 1940. Russell, born May 18, 1872, has made contributions to mathematical logic, mathematics, the philosophy of science, and social and political philosophy that have established him among the foremost living philosophers in the English-speaking world. "Bertrand Russell," wrote Rudolf Metz, "is the only British thinker of the age

---

[1] This paper was first published in *Twice a Year*, issue V–VI, November 1940. It has been revised and corrected and brought up to date.

who has an international reputation; the only one whose name is known in all countries. To this extent he has succeeded to the inheritance of Spencer." [2]

Unlike Spencer, Russell is a member of the British nobility. His father was Viscount Amberley; his grandfather was Lord John Russell, in whose household he was brought up. He has inherited the title of Earl Russell, but prefers professionally to use the name by which he is known as a writer. He has, however, enlarged and enriched the democratic disposition which is also a part of his inheritance. His grandfather brought about the repeal of the English Test and Corporation Acts which barred from public office anyone not a member of his own Church of England, and thus extended political equality to religious minorities, of whom the Catholics were the most numerous group. Russell's social and political teachings might be described as a scientific justification of the general process of liberation and equalization of which his grandfather's act was a part.

His intellectual beginnings were all in logic and mathematics, and his writings on those subjects are regarded as among the most significant in the contemporary world. The First World War brought home to him the problems of human relations, which had been until then rather abstract and intellectual to his mind, in a personal and passionate way. He was a pacifist. Many of his readers thought him to be a through and through one. But he believed that some wars are just, and he opposed the First World War on particular, not on general grounds. In 1918 he published an article in which he quoted, in support of his opposition, from an official United States publication instances of the use of United States troops in quelling labor disputes. The quotation was held, under the Defense of the Realm Act, to be

---

[2] *A Hundred Years of British Philosophy*, New York, 1938.

prejudicial to Anglo-American relations, and Russell was imprisoned for four and a half months. While in jail he wrote his *Introduction to Mathematical Philosophy*.

He had married young, and after many years of a childless marriage he and his first wife separated. A second marriage, of which there were two children, was dissolved in 1935. Around the children of this second marriage the Russells created, in 1927, a progressive experimental school which eventually they could not keep up because it cost too much. Russell entered upon a third marriage in 1936. His divorces were attended with the usual difficulties which English law and the Church of England impose, admitting as they do only adultery as ground for divorce. The hypocritical cruelty of canonically controlled civil law is well known and only ecclesiastic interests take it seriously.

Russell's standing as a man, a scientist, a philosopher, surely remains unaffected by whether he has been divorced or not. His fame is world-wide. He is the holder of the Nicholas Murray Butler Medal of Columbia University, the Sylvester Medal of the Royal Society, and the de Morgan Medal of the London Mathematical Society. He is an Honorary Member of the Reale Accademia dei Lincei. He has been Fellow and Lecturer of Trinity College, Cambridge, Herbert Spencer Lecturer at Oxford, Visiting Professor of Philosophy at Harvard University and at the Chinese Government University of Peking, Tarner Lecturer at Cambridge University, Special Lecturer at the London School of Economics and Political Science and at the University of Oxford, Visiting Professor of Philosophy at the University of Chicago, Professor of Philosophy at the University of California at Los Angeles, occasional lecturer at the universities of Upsala, Copenhagen, and Barcelona, at the Sorbonne, etc.

Such is the man and philosopher to whom the chairman of the Board of Higher Education had written on February 29, 1940:

My dear Professor Russell:

It is with a deep sense of privilege that I take this opportunity of notifying you of your appointment as Professor of Philosophy at the City College for the period February 1, 1941, to June 30, 1942, pursuant to action taken by the Board of Higher Education at its meeting of February 26, 1940 (Calendar No. 14-b).

I know that your acceptance of this appointment will add luster to the name and achievements of the Department and College and that it will deepen and extend the interest of the College in the philosophic bases of human living.

Yours very sincerely,

This same man and philosopher, a few months later, was pronounced by a New York judge unworthy to be Professor of Philosophy at the College of the City of New York.

II

"The Russell Case" itself developed in the following manner:

On February 26, 1940, the Board of Higher Education of New York City, by a unanimous vote, named Bertrand Russell to be Professor of Philosophy at the College of the City of New York for eighteen months, beginning with the Fall Term of 1941.

The College of the City of New York is one of the four collegiate institutions maintained by New York City for the education of children of its citizens. Of these four, two, Brooklyn College and Queens College, are co-educational; one, Hunter College, is exclusively for girls; the College of the City of New York is exclusively for boys in its day sessions.

[18]

Bertrand Russell was appointed to teach senior and junior male undergraduates the following specific subjects:

1. Logic and its relation to science, mathematics, and philosophy.
2. Problems in the foundations of mathematics.
3. Relations of the pure to applied sciences and the reciprocal influence of metaphysics and scientific theories.

When the appointment was made public, William T. Manning, a bishop of the Protestant Episcopal Church, wrote a letter to the press denouncing the appointment on the ground that Mr. Russell is "a recognized propagandist against religion and morality and who specifically defends adultery."

It was generally assumed that the clergyman was speaking for his Church. But a fellow-clergyman, the editor of the *Churchman,* Dr. Guy Emery Shipler, hastened to point out:

Bishop Manning has been given no authority to represent the Protestant Episcopal Church in such controversies. He is one voice, and only one, out of a million and a half communicants. He has every right to speak for himself; he has no right to speak either for his own diocese or for the national church. He cannot speak even for the episcopate, of which he is one among 153. No authority has been given him to represent either the House of Bishops or his diocesan convention in this matter. Only the General Convention, composed of bishops and other clergy and laymen, could authorize him to speak for the Episcopal Church. It is unfortunate that the public is under the illusion that every time a bishop, particularly a bishop of a metropolitan diocese, bursts into print with a point of view stemming from the Dark Ages he represents the Protestant Episcopal Church.[3]

---

[3] *New Republic,* April 8, 1940.

Following the clergyman's letter, attacks on the appointment came in numbers. The attacks were consistently of ecclesiastical and political origin. Among them was the unsuccessful endeavor of a member of the Board of Higher Education, a communicant of Bishop Manning's and a Republican politician, to have the philosopher's appointment rescinded by the Board. This having failed, the assault was finally given effective form by the filing of a proceeding by a taxpayer's suit in the New York Supreme Court to vacate the appointment of Bertrand Russell on the ground that he was an alien and an advocate of sexual immorality. The suit was initiated in the name of a Mrs. Jean Kay of Brooklyn, who declared that she was afraid of what might happen to her daughter if she were a student at the boys' College of the City of New York and Bertrand Russell were teaching there the philosophy of mathematics and of science. Representing Mrs. Jean Kay before the court was a lawyer named Joseph Goldstein, who, when Tammany and its affiliates were in power in New York City, had held office as a city magistrate. This ex-magistrate's brief described Bertrand Russell's works in terms that not even the most unfriendly critics, in all the years that Russell had been writing, ever dreamed of using about them. Goldstein called them "lecherous, salacious, libidinous, lustful, venerous, erotomaniac, aphrodisiac, atheistic, irreverent, narrow-minded, untruthful, and bereft of moral fiber." He also charged that the philosopher had gone in for salacious poetry, had maintained an English nudist colony, had condoned homosexuality, that, moreover, he was not a citizen. Goldstein added:

He is not a philosopher in the accepted meaning of the word; not a lover of wisdom; not a searcher after wisdom; not an explorer of that universal science which aims at the explanation

[20]

of all the phenomena of the universe by ultimate causes; that in the opinion of your deponent and multitudes of other persons he is a sophist; practices sophism; that by cunning contrivances, tricks, and devices, and by mere quibbling, he puts forth fallacious arguments and arguments that are not supported by sound reasoning; and he draws inferences which are not justly deduced from a sound premise; that all his alleged doctrines which he calls philosophy are just cheap, tawdry, worn out, patched up fetishes and propositions, devises for the purpose of misleading the people.

The judge before whom this plea was made was a John E. McGeehan, a Roman Catholic, a graduate of local Catholic schools; he was backed by the Bronx Democratic political machine associated with Tammany; he had last distinguished himself by trying to have a portrait of Martin Luther removed from a court-house mural illustrating legal history. The Jesuit periodical *America* says his Honor reads Horace, a poet not unknown for his salacity and praise of homosexuality. The Board of Higher Education was represented by Nicholas Bucci, Assistant Corporation Counsel. Bucci's reply to Goldstein confined itself to the only legally relevant point in the latter's petition; viz., that a noncitizen could not be appointed to a post in a city college. Mr. Bucci argued that this was not the case, and asked for dismissal of the suit.

To this McGeehan replied: "If I find that these books sustain the allegations of the petition, I will give the Appellate Division and the Court of Appeals something to think about." [4]

On March 30 the justice made public the intellectual exercise he had promised to give the higher courts of the State of New York. It was a very long document, based, its

[4] *New York Herald Tribune*, March 28, 1940.

author claimed, on "normae and criteria . . . which are the laws of nature and nature's God." According to the *New Republic*, it must have been "produced at superhuman speed if the justice actually wrote it after all the evidence was in." It voided the appointment on three main grounds: two purely technical, which would invalidate the appointment of any distinguished foreign or indeed any teacher of established reputation who might be unwilling to take a civil service examination; the other, according to the justice, "compelling." He said he had to void the appointment because it "adversely affects public health, safety, and morals"; because it would "aid, abet, or encourage any course of conduct tending to a violation of the penal law." The Board, he said, had no right to appoint an alien to a teaching post in the city, nor without testing his competency in a competitive examination. Nor had it only thus gone beyond its powers in appointing Bertrand Russell; it had in effect established a "chair of indecency" at the City College. He not only said that Russell's teachings are calculated to encourage violations of the State's penal law. He said that the Board of Higher Education has "moral standards lower than common decency requires." He also said that "academic freedom is freedom to do good, not freedom to teach evil." Later he added that he had had to take a bath after reading one of the philosopher's books.

One consequence of the agitation was a vituperative public assault upon the members of the Board of Higher Education which split its ranks. A fundamentalist—Catholic and Protestant—minority aligned themselves with Episcopalian Tuttle. The rest remained faithful to their convictions. They voted to appeal Mr. McGeehan's decision. This vote, however justified on grounds of personal integrity, public duty, and administrative responsibility, was politically very inconvenient to the city administration, continually harassed by Tammany office-holders in its midst. The reform Mayor of New York City, Fiorello La Guardia, attempted to dismiss the issue which the vote raised, by striking from the budget the position to which Bertrand Russell had been appointed, and his Corporation Counsel, W. C. Chanler, advised the Board that he declined to take an appeal because he feared "that the religious and moral controversies" involved would blind the courts to the vicious wider effects of the McGeehan decision and to the legal principles underlying.

In this opinion of the courts the Board of Higher Education declined to concur. It had more faith in their integrity, and undertook to appeal. Messrs. Buckner and Harlan of the firm of Root, Clark, Buckner, and Ballantine volunteered their services as counsel, without fee. Every effort was made to smother this appeal through private counsel. McGeehan denied the counsel's motion for permission to make the appeal. The denial was immediately taken to the Appellate Court, composed largely of Roman Catholics. This court refused to accept briefs from the Lawyers' Guild, the Bertrand Russell Committee, the Committee for Cultural Freedom, the College Teachers' Union, and the Women's City Club as friends of the court, but did agree to accept such briefs from Mr. Tuttle and his few associates on the Board who were opposing the majority.

When Mrs. Kay brought the proceeding to have the courts revoke Russell's appointment she did not make Russell himself a party to that proceeding. Nor had Russell been officially notified of the institution of the proceeding by the Board of Higher Education. However, informed by friends of the manner in which the proceeding was being defended by the Corporation Counsel acting for the Board of Higher Education, Russell felt an obligation to become a

[2 3]

party to the proceeding and be represented by independent counsel. He retained for that purpose Osmond K. Fraenkel, who was suggested to him by the American Civil Liberties Union. Mr. Fraenkel is a director of the Union.

On the day following the announcement of the decision by Mr. Justice McGeehan, and before any order was entered on that decision, Mr. Fraenkel, on Russell's behalf, applied to McGeehan to have Russell made a party to the proceeding and for permission to Russell to file an answer challenging the scandalous charges made against him. This application the justice characteristically denied on the ground that Russell had no legal interest in the proceedings.[5] The *New York Times* editorially deprecated his de-

---

[5] This decision was taken to the Appellate Division of the Supreme Court for the First Judicial Department on Appeal. That court unanimously upheld Mr. Justice McGeehan, but wrote no opinion explaining its reason for so doing. Permission was then asked of the Appellate Division for the carrying of an appeal to the Court of Appeals and that permission was denied. Mr. Fraenkel then took the last step available to him under the circumstances and applied to the Court of Appeals for permission to appeal. This application came on while the court was in recess. When it reconvened in October, it refused to grant the application on the ground that the lower court's order denying intervention was not a final one. Thereupon Mr. Fraenkel sought a review of the case by appealing the final order which vacated Mr. Russell's appointment. But in January 1941 the Court of Appeals denied his application for leave to appeal from the Appellate Division's decision rejecting Mr. Russell's appeal and thus estopped the latter from any further effort to seek justice through the law courts.

The appeal of Messrs. Harlan and Buckner on behalf of the Board of Higher Education fared no better. The Appellate Division, in refusing it, did not pass on the correctness of McGeehan's order nullifying the philosopher's appointment. It confined its judgment solely to the medium of the appeal, holding that the Corporation Counsel alone could be that medium. Inasmuch as the latter had refused to take the appeal, no one else might, and those taken by Messrs. Buckner and Harlan on behalf of the Board and of the individual members of the Board's majority were accordingly dismissed. Meanwhile, Mr. Russell had been invited to join the Barnes Foundation, and the Board found it convenient to take no further steps in defense of its own lawful powers and functions.

This is the first case on record where a court stepped in to void an ap-

fending himself; he should, it said, "have had the wisdom to retire from the appointment as soon as its harmful effects became evident."

Bertrand Russell did not, however, feel free to withdraw, as the *Times* suggested. Even if a man of his fame and standing ever could have been an anonymous teacher appointed to a teaching post, William Manning's assault, Joseph Goldstein's accusation, McGeehan's judicial affirmation of the accusation, changed the philosopher's status. They made his cause the public cause of administrative autonomy for appointive bodies and of academic freedom for the teaching professions. The ecclesiastic's personal attack upon Mr. Russell and its court-room sequelae had been followed by series of attacks and denunciations by individuals and groups with various labels but with a common politico-ecclesiastical animus. The leading individuals were the Republican politician George U. Harvey, president of the Borough of Queens; the Democratic politicians James J. Lyons, president of the Borough of the Bronx, and Michael F. Walsh, Secretary of New York State; Mayor Frank Hague's master of Chancery Courts Matthews, an alleged anti-English pro-Nazi radio propagandist; the priest Edward Lodge Curran, president of the International Catholic Truth Society, associated with the notorious Christian Front and allied to the Fascist priest Charles Coughlin of Detroit. Among the organizations were various Catholic Holy Name Societies, councils of the Knights of Columbus; the Guild of Catholic Lawyers; the Sons of Xavier, lodges of the Ancient Order of Hibernians, National Catholic Alumnae Association, the Newman Club of the College of the

---

pointment by a board of education on petition of a single citizen, or denied to a school board the right to engage private counsel and to the appointee involved the right to a hearing.

[2 5]

City of New York, and William Randolph Hearst. Among the Protestants who aligned themselves with Manning and Goldstein were the clergymen H. Darlington, N. V. Peale, Miller Ritchie, the Greater New York Federation of Churches, and the Metropolitan Baptist Ministers' Conference. The Midwest Conference of the Society of New England Women, the Empire State Sons of the American Revolution, and the New York County American Legion seem to have been the only formally secular groups.

As against this combination of fundamentalist clerics, machine politicians, and professional patriots, there rushed to the defense of the powers and personality of Bertrand Russell, of his moral and intellectual integrity, of his courage and his devotion to the cause of truth and of his value as a teacher, scholars, scientists, clergymen, and laymen of all views and opinions. Most of them do not agree with him, either in metaphysics or in ethics. They all endorsed him: Alfred North Whitehead, the sage at Harvard; John Dewey, the foremost philosopher of America; Albert Einstein, Oswald Veblen, Harlow Shapley, Edward Kasner, leaders in mathematical physics, mathematics, and astronomy; the nation's leading philosophers: Professors Montague, Ducasse, Hook, Perry, Randall, Cohen, Lovejoy, and many others; the presidents of colleges and universities —institutions of higher learning where Russell had taught, is teaching, or will teach, as well as others: Sproul of California, Hutchins of Chicago, Neilson of Smith, Gideonse of Brooklyn, Alexander of Antioch, Graham of North Carolina, McAfee of Wellesley; the presidents and past presidents of the learned societies: Nicholson, of the Phi Beta Kappa; Curry, of the American Mathematical Association; Hankins, of the American Sociological Association; Beard, of the American Historical Association; Allport, of the

[2 6]

American Psychological Association; Ducasse, of the American Philosophical Association; Himstead, of the American Association of University Professors; and many others.

Among the ministers of religion who defended Russell were Edgar S. Brightman, Director, National Council on Religion in Education; Rev. Robert G. Andrus, counselor to Protestant Students in Columbia University; Rev. John Haynes Holmes, Community Church, New York City; Rev. John Paul Jones; Rev. Hartley J. Hartmann; Dr. Henry Neumann, Director, Brooklyn Society for Ethical Culture; Rabbi Jonah B. Wise; Rev. A. J. Muste, Labor Temple (Presbyterian), New York City; the Liberal Ministers Club of New York City; Professor H. E. Luccock, Yale Divinity School; Professor J. S. Bixler, Harvard Divinity School. Add to these the Alumni Associations of the College of the City of New York and of Brooklyn College, the American Law Students' Association, the students at the University of California at Los Angeles who were at the time in Mr. Russell's classes, the Willard Straight Post of the American Legion, the Women's City Club of New York, and Newbold Morris, president of the City Council, member of the Rev. Mr. Manning's church.

The ecclesiastical assault on Mr. Russell in New York led to emulative efforts elsewhere.

In California, at whose State university in Los Angeles the philosopher was then teaching, a suit like Joseph Goldstein's was brought by one I. R. Wall, a Baptist clergyman without a pulpit. The courts threw out the case.

In Massachusetts, Thomas Dorgan, Catholic Democratic politician without office, demanded that Harvard University should rescind the appointment of Bertrand Russell to be William James Lecturer in Philosophy for 1940. The University replied: "The president and fellows have taken

[2 7]

cognizance of the criticism of this appointment. After reviewing all the circumstances, they have considered it to be for the best interests of the University to reaffirm their decision and they have done so."

Chancellor Chase, of New York University, a vestryman of Trinity Church in Bishop Manning's diocese, declared in a letter to the *New York Times* that if the McGeehan affirmation of the Goldstein libel be upheld, "a blow has been struck at the security and intellectual independence of every faculty member in every public college and university in the United States." If upheld, the decision would, "given a taxpayer's suit, empower a court to void a faculty appointment on account of an individual's opinions." The consequences, wrote the Chancellor, were "incalculable." [6]

Others—the metropolitan press and its columnists, clergymen, laymen, educators—were of a similar opinion. The *Herald Tribune* said editorially: "There is now a Russell case to which no friend of civil liberty and academic freedom can remain indifferent. There was not before." Dorothy Thompson wrote: [7]

Lord Russell emerges . . . as a twentieth-century Socrates, with the Bishop brandishing the cup of hemlock in his face. No evidence is presented that Lord Russell has ever corrupted anyone; no evidence is presented that his views on marriage and morals have had the slightest effect on the tendencies of the times; no evidence is presented that he has ever wrecked anybody's life by his own practices. He has been divorced, twice I believe, but so no doubt have some members of Bishop Manning's diocese and probably of his congregation, and I doubt whether the Bishop has thrown them out of the fold or publicly excoriated them.

---

[6] *New York Times*, April 20, 1940.
[7] "On the Record," *New York Herald Tribune*, March 27, 1940.

Apparently the important thing is not what people do, but what they say. For if the church—in the good old tradition of *The Scarlet Letter*—were to excommunicate all who do not strictly follow its teachings regarding sexual morality, it would become a diminished society, and could hardly support either the plant or the priesthood that it does.

Now, this is not an argument against Bishop Manning's views. It is an argument against the attempt to destroy the professional life of a distinguished scholar because he voices opinions which are, in fact, the actual practices of a part of our most respected population. Lord Russell is not immoral. Anyone who knows him is aware that he is a man of the most exquisite intellectual and personal integrity.

The issue, if it had ever been personal, had ceased to be so. Replying to its editorial, Mr. Russell wrote the *New York Times:* [8]

. . . If I had considered only my own interests and inclinations I should have retired at once. But however wise such action might have been from a personal point of view, it would also, in my judgment, have been cowardly and selfish. A great many people who realized that their own interests and the principles of toleration and free speech were at stake were anxious from the first to continue the controversy. If I had retired I should have robbed them of their *casus belli* and tacitly assented to the proposition that substantial groups shall be allowed to drive out of public office individuals whose opinions, race, or nationality they find repugnant. This to me would appear immoral.

To Bishop Manning, that the issue should be met in this way, that the foremost ethical and intellectual leaders in American life should stand by Russell, was "sinister." "If," he mouthed, "the heads of any of our colleges and universities countenance men like Russell—and the grave fact

[8] April 26, 1940.

is that some of them do—it is time for the Christian Church and for all who believe in God and the moral law to make an open issue."

III

The ecclesiastic is consistent. His knowledge of the Christian Church is as belated as his ideas about God and the moral law. The issue, so novel to the Bishop, has been open since Jesus of Nazareth opened it against the Temple priestcraft of Judea two thousand years ago. It is the issue of the Waldenses against Innocent IV; of the Franciscan Spirituals against John XXII; of John Huss against the Council of Constance; of Joan of Arc against the Inquisition of Rouen; of Jews, Moors, and heretics against Torquemada; of Savonarola against Borgian Pope Alexander VI; of Martin Luther against Leo X; of Servetus against John Calvin. It is the issue of the Protestant Reformation against the religious imperialism of the Papacy. It is the issue, within Protestantism, of the liberty of the individual conscience against corporate coercion. It is the issue, within the enclaves of Christian culture, of religious and secular free thought against priestly domination of thought. In sum, it is the issue of free religion against the dogmatic theology of ecclesiastics; it is the issue of the open competitive method of scientific inquiry against the closed monopolistic indoctrinations of ecclesiasticism.

The ecclesiastical assault on Bertrand Russell is but the current phase of a warfare waged by priestcraft against men of faith and science since science first began to penetrate the dogmatic walls of churchly doctrine. The aggressors in this warfare have been the churchmen, not the scientists. There exists, it is true, a widespread notion that it is science which wages a war upon religion, but that notion is a consequence of ecclesiastical propaganda, without any basis in the record. Men of science have been invariably men of deep religious feeling, marked by a piety and devotion to their faiths rarely equaled among professional religionists. Many of them have been themselves churchmen: personalities like Albertus Magnus, Roger Bacon, Copernicus, Nicolaus of Cusa, Giordano Bruno, Mendel, Renan, Robertson Smith, Colenso, Bartolo, Lenormant, Loisy. Others have been consecrated laymen like Galileo and Kepler and Newton, like Lyell and Darwin, like Eddington, Millikan, and Jeans, like William James and John Dewey, Albert Einstein and Alfred North Whitehead. Bertrand Russell himself, as every reader of *A Free Man's Worship* or *The Principles of Social Reconstruction* or, for that matter, *Marriage and Morals* knows, is a man of a deeply religious cast of mind. Each such man endeavors to see the world truly and to see it whole. Some continue to call the whole "God," others call it "Nature," all add new discoveries to old insights, all set unprecedented observations beside doctrines sanctified by tradition and grounded in habit. Those doctrines are orthodoxy; an innovation is heresy. To accept the latter would be to admit that the traditional and habitual is not the universal and eternal, to acquiesce in the disagreeable task of continually readjusting and modifying dogma into harmony with new observation and discovery. The idea of "God" or of "Nature" with which a Whitehead or an Einstein, a Dewey or an Eddington, ends his inquiry, is consequently not the same as the idea with which he begins his inquiry. Old elements have been abandoned; new ones have been added; the whole has been reshaped. And what is true regarding such general ideas as "God" or "Nature" is even truer regarding the specific ideas and data of which the sciences of matter, of life, and of man consist.

[3 1]

Such continual transformation of the old in the light of the new the official keepers of any orthodox "deposit of faith" resent and reject. When Kepler, a pious soul and loyal Catholic, said of his astronomical conceptions: "I do think the thoughts of God," he was assigning God other thoughts than churchmen and inquisitors declared to be the correct ones. When Charles Darwin demonstrated the origin of species and described the descent of man, when Sir Charles Lyell exhibited the antiquity of the earth, when Colenso, Anglican Bishop of Natal, brought the Bible into the conspectus of common sense and science, they also assigned to God and to Nature other thoughts and other methods than those approved of for God and for Nature by the dead men speaking with authority for the Anglican bishop, Manning, for the Roman Catholic judge, McGeehan, and for the Judaistic ex-judge, Goldstein. That the Church cannot err in matters of faith and morals is a claim common to Roman Catholicism and High Anglicanism. Roman Catholicism later developed this into the claim of papal infallibility.

To keep their notions about God and Nature from the competition of others, the persecutors of Bertrand Russell, like their fathers before them, are continuing the two wars which make up the bulk of the history of religions. They are waging a *civil war* against new religions, new cults, new sects and their "heresies." They are waging a *foreign w* against science. They are waging these wars because they wish, where they already have it, to maintain, and, where they do not have it, to impose, their sole and exclusive rule of the minds and hearts of men. They demand monopoly, and will brook no competition.

But religious heresies and scientific ideas *are* competition. They arise because the orthodox system has failed to do its job, and they are endeavors to do that same job better. The job is called by churchmen Salvation; it goes by other names in other enclaves; but whatever the name, it stands for the same task, the same end: to enable men to be freer and safer and happier whether in this world or another. Orthodoxies are more concerned with another world; heresies and science with this world. But all alike recognize that the world we now live in is not a world that was made for us; that it is a world beset with dangers, threatening hunger and thirst and cold, sickness and barrenness, warfare and death. Religion and science both figure as instruments in mankind's struggle to live and to grow and to be at peace in this world, as agencies wherewith to secure an abundance of food, clothing, and shelter, assurance of offspring, protection from disease, victory in battle, conquest over death. They do this by means of ideas regarding the origin, the nature, and the history of the world and of man; and by making up, on the basis of these ideas, devices with which to manipulate and control, to alter and direct, both men and events in such a way as to destroy what is held to be evil and to further what is held to be good. In a word, both science and religion are endeavors to discern the causes and to control the consequences of events, to define rules of conduct and to determine ways of life which shall accomplish the salvation men desire: they set up ends and designate the means to those ends.

The causes, the consequences, are not things seen. They are things unseen, which belong to the past which is no more or to the future which is not yet, and are referred to a locus beyond the reach of our senses and transcending the events of the daily life. In this common enterprise religion is far older than science. Its theory of causes and of ends and means is no less older. This theory is usually called supernaturalist, anthropomorphic. Where science speaks of energy, electrons, protons, space-time, light-years, and the like, traditional religions speak of gods, devils, angels, spirits, heaven, hell: more recent and heretical ones assign the causes of things to such anthropomorphic supernaturalisms as the Dialectical Materialism of the Bolsheviks, the Race of the Nazis, the Totalitarian State of the Fascists.

Religions—the godly and the godless alike—differ from science not so much, however, in *what* they believe to be the unseen cause and rule of the world, as in *how* they establish and prove their beliefs; and in *how* they manipulate and control the objects of their beliefs. Thus, religion grounds its beliefs upon some initial revelation, transmits them by authority, and imposes them by force. It asserts that they are universal, eternal and unalterable, exempt from any doubt or challenge, endowed with an absolute and exclusive claim to the allegiance of the human mind. To manipulate and control the gods, angels, devils, and the other objects of religious belief, churchmen, who are professionals specially trained to these occupations, are employed to say prayers, perform rituals and ceremonies, and repeat and enforce prescriptions and taboos regarding personal conduct. These techniques are declared to be able to accomplish anything: to bring rain, cure disease, overcome barrenness, prosper the friend, defeat the foe, ease the imputed torments of the dead, and obviate the consequences of ecclesiastically forbidden conduct by the living. Since these techniques and the ideas upon which they are based recurrently disappoint the believers, the latter search out new ideas, devise different techniques, and protest the old and their claims. Such actions constitute heresies. To prevent their arising and to suppress them when they do arise, churchmen claim that they, and they alone, are commissioned by God to teach

[34]

what is true doctrine and right conduct, and they demand control of education. "As a mandate to teach," said Pope Pius XI, "Christ conferred infallibility in educative work on his church."

Now, where religion grounds its doctrines on unique, mysterious revelation, science elicits its ideas from the ordinary experiences of the daily life; where religion transmits dogmas on authority and imposes them by force, science continually checks and tests its theories or laws by observations and experiments; where religion refuses to consider alternatives and seeks to impose its dogmas to the exclusion of all others, science welcomes alternatives and invites competition of ideas and procedures. Where religion begins with a dogma finished, unalterable, infallible, science does so with a hypothesis, which it continually subjects to modification and improvement in the light of experiment and new knowledge. The result is that the history of religion presents itself as a multiplication of mutually exclusive heresies and sects, each with its own infallible revelation: the history of science presents a multitude of alternatives, each with an equal claim to truth, coming together in an ever completer harmonization and unity, moving toward a consensus which rests on the free consent of all the scientists concerned with the initial differences. The making of this consensus may be observed, both in the theoretical sciences and in the applied sciences, be they physics, chemistry, engineering, biology, agriculture, medicine, or mathematics.

Wherever salvation is sought chiefly by the methods of science and by the technologies based on science, men are freer, healthier, better fed, happier, more peaceable, and live longer. Wherever salvation is sought chiefly by the methods of religion and the technologies based on religion, the opposite is the case. The contrast during the past hundred years between the lives and labors of the peoples of France and England, the Scandinavian countries and the United States, with those of Spain, Portugal, Poland, Russia, India, Hitler Germany, and Fascist Italy, points the moral. On the record, wherever science has had an opportunity to compete freely with religion in doing any specific job, it has, on the whole and in the long run, done the job better. This is why people speak of "the religion of Science."

Of course, persons who make their livings out of religion are much put out. Unchecked, the employment of scientific ideas and techniques would have the same effect on ecclesiasticism as the employment of the railroad and the motor-car had on the horse and buggy. And it is true, as the priestcraft continually complain, that men give less heed to what *they* call religion than they used to. Some sects, in order to compete with science, adopt the faith, the attitudes, the methods, and the techniques of science, insisting only that the word "God" and sentiments and symbols centered on it be retained. These are the modernists of the Catholic dispensation, the progressives of the Protestant; and the latter far outnumber the former. Most sects, however, concede nothing and demand all. They attribute every ill mankind is suffering from to neglect of *their* religion, without regard to the fact that human ills are not fewer nor different from what they were before science, and that human goods, spiritual and material, are more abundant, more diversified, and more secure than they were before science. They complain bitterly of the neglect of the church, demand that its use should be spread by other means than its inward merit, insist on the absolute and exclusive prerogative of their occupation to employment and reverence. Dr. Harry Emerson Fosdick has pointed out the anomaly:

[3 6]

Nobody solicitously is trying to save science, for the simple reason that in its own sphere science is saving us. . . . Science is not yet an organization to be maintained or a final creed to be preserved; it is still in the creative vigor of individual venturesomeness and exploration. . . . Turn, however, to religion! . . . Multitudes of people are out with props trying to shore up religion . . . until the impression prevails that the major business of churchmen is to keep religion going.

The methods employed by the Anglican churchman, Manning, the Catholic judge, McGeehan, the Judaist lawyer, Goldstein, and their churchly associates against Bertrand Russell's appointment to teach mathematical philosophy at the College of the City of New York is the current scientific sample of the methods generally employed by churchmen "to keep religion going." They are methods which are condemned in sport and impossible in science, art, or true religion. They are not uncommon, but are treated as unlawful—although the law is a mighty shelter for such methods—in business, and on occasion government prosecutes businessmen accused of employing them, businessmen charged with being monopolists or would-be monopolists, engaged in "unfair competition." When such methods occur in sport they are called "fouling." Sportsmanship or fair competition consists in equal opportunity to demonstrate excellence; it consists in refusing any handicap or privilege in the competition with rivals to perform a feat, to do a service, to accomplish a work, to achieve an end; it consists of being willing and ready to win or lose on one's merits, without fear or favor.

Until the insurgence of the Bolsheviks, the Fascists, and the Nazis, no traditional occupation except the ecclesiastical had openly and boldly demanded exemption from the rules of fair competition and claimed unfair competition as a right and fouling as a religious duty. Now those godless cults have joined the godly ones in making these claims. The Nazis are explicit about it. "The Third Reich," wrote the Nazi of Catholic faith, Franz von Papen, in the *Völkischer Beobachter* of January 14, 1934, "is the first power which not only recognizes but which puts into practice the high principles of the Papacy." In this he was unjust to both the Bolsheviks and the Fascists, who antedated the Nazis in that emulation. The priestcraft of each cult, godless and godly alike, lay claim to be the keepers of a unique, infallible "deposit of faith" revealed to them alone, which they are charged by the Triune God or by Dialectical Materialism or by Metaphysical Aryan Blood, or by the Total Act which is the Fascist State, to impose on the rest of mankind. They assert that God and Destiny command that humanity shall believe without doubt, obey without protest, serve without hesitation. Each cult arrogates to its doctrine and discipline the exclusive privilege it claims to be the due of infallibility: "I am right," each says to the others, and to the rest of the world, "and you are wrong; when you are in power it is your duty to tolerate me because I am right; when I am in power it is my duty to persecute you because you are wrong."

IV

By and large, but with a growing number of exceptions to be found almost exclusively in the Protestant world, such as the Quakers, the churchmen have remained zealous in their "duty to persecute." Since their infallible "deposit of faith" revealed not only the will of God regarding man, but the entire history, structure, and action of the universe,

[38]

of its inanimate matter, and of its living forms, they persecuted the different wherever they found it: in astronomy,
in physics, in biology, in history, in archaeology, in philol-
ogy. . . . Readers of Andrew D. White's *History of the
Warfare of Science with Theology* [9] will remember how
each step in the progress of the positive sciences was attended with ecclesiastical suppression and ecclesiastical ven-
geance. Never was there on the part of ecclesiastical authority any undertaking to examine the new idea or the new
technique on its merits, to check it by observation, or to
verify it by experiment. Consistently, churchmen instead
endeavored to silence the ideas' author, to assassinate his
character, to burn his living body and the books in which he
had written his ideas down, to inscribe them in an Index
Prohibitory or Expurgatory, and with due penalties to forbid persons within reach of ecclesiastical power to read
them. Consistently, churchmen set up devices to prevent
new ideas, variants, possible heresies from arising; or if
arisen, from being published and circulated. They set up
censorships, which prevail and operate to this day, and
which the totalitarian cults in Germany, Russia, Spain, and
Italy emulate without improving upon. They set up an Inquisition commissioned by torture and fire to eliminate all
variation from their infallible prescriptions. Lord Acton
wrote to Mary Gladstone: [10] "The principle of the Inquisition is murderous, and a man's opinion of the Papacy is regu-
lated by his opinions about religious assassination." The
Roman Catholic Church maintains Censorship, Index, and
Inquisition to this day. Other sects, that would if they could,
make use instead of slander and calumny, political influence

[9] New York, 1896, 2 vols.
[10] *Letters to Mary Gladstone*, London, 1905, p. 105.

[39]

and social pressure. None is concerned about the scientific correctness of an idea or the social value of a method. All are concerned with preserving their monopolies by maiming or destroying the competitor.

Since the ecclesiastical murder, by burning, of Giordano Bruno, torture of Galileo, vendetta against Newton, workers in the astronomical and physical sciences have been left in relative peace by churchmen. True, an Irish Catholic Cardinal has denounced relativity, about which he knows less than nothing, because he suspected it might make for atheism—which to him is the same as a conception of God other than his own—but the condemnation has not been institutional. The institutional condemnation of relativity on doctrinal grounds came from the Nazis and the Bolsheviks. The latter have also condemned Mendelian genetics. Since the calumniation of Darwin by highly placed clerics of the Church of England, ecclesiastical condemnation of evolutionary biology has been sporadic and intermittent, and the same holds for medicine and mental hygiene. It might be said that the churchmen have to a considerable degree retreated from those fields. But in two fields they fight an entrenched warfare. One is the field of biblical criticism, church history and philosophy. The other is the field of social science. They call the first field "faith"; the second, "morals." They bitterly dispute the ground in all the disciplines affecting the infallibility and unalterability of the dogmas of the faith; and regarding all that affects folkways and mores, especially sexways, they are as fanatical and cruel as they dare to be.

Scientific method in religious inquiry is especially obnoxious to the Catholics. "The modern mind," Gregory XVI declared in the encyclical *Singulari Nos*, "seeks to know beyond what it is meant to know . . . relying too much on itself, thinks it can find the truth outside the Catholic Church wherein truth is found without the slightest shadow of error." In 1864 Pio Nono appended to the encyclical *Quanta Cura* a "Syllabus of 80 Modern Errors" which directly or by implication enumerated and proscribed practically every advance the sciences had made, while the encyclical condemned all those who did not acknowledge papal infallibility. Leo XIII consistently persecuted Catholic scholars such as Döllinger. In 1885, he declared in the encyclical *Immortali Dei* that all Catholics must believe whatever the Roman Pontiffs affirmed, especially as regards modern liberties. The encyclical *Sapientiae Christianae* re-affirmed this, requiring obedience not only to dogmatic decisions but to all the instructions of the hierarchy and especially of the Pope. Pius X made the Catholic warfare against scientific method in the study of religion and church history one of extermination. Confirming the Decree of the Holy Roman and Universal Inquisition which condemned and proscribed the autonomy of science and the validity of its methods, he condemned views come by in this way as Modernism, which he described as the "synthesis of all the heresies." Persons tainted with Modernism were to be excommunicated, censorship was to be extended and intensified, and a secret council of vigilance against Modernism was to be set up. Biblical scholarship, higher criticism and the social sciences have made their greatest advances in the enclaves of the Protestant churches, not excluding the Anglican and Episcopal. Those churches have their fundamentalists, but as a whole they neither arrogate to themselves infallibility nor the exclusive possession of the "Truth and the Way."

[41]

But it is in the field of the social sciences or "morals" that the ecclesiastical interests have their greatest strength and receive the strongest support for their claim that their dogmas regarding property, both human and chattel, sex-relations, marriage and divorce, birth control and sex-education, are infallible. On these issues, too, Protestantism has been far readier to learn from science. No Protestant theologian, for example, any longer justifies slavery, but it is the teaching of St. Thomas Aquinas that slavery is economically sound and morally defensible. Thomas Aquinas is currently much in vogue. He is the official theologian of the Roman Catholic Church. The submissive and undoubting study of his works is prescribed by various papal encyclicals, and commanded by the encyclical *Pascendi Gregis*.

But it is regarding matters of sex that the churchmen have been most aggressive and most intransigent in claiming for their dogmas the special privileges of immunity from doubt, inquiry, and competition. It is because of his scientific findings on these matters that Bertrand Russell is assaulted in the characteristic manner of churchmen. Russell, after an extraordinarily wide examination of the literature in the field, and after extensive observation and analysis of sexual behavior, arrived at certain opinions on these matters which are different from the dogmas of the churches. He had analyzed not only the objective studies of generations of historians, anthropologists, psychologists, psychiatrists, economists, sociologists, physicians, and intellectually honest churchmen; he had also studied the relevant works of the early church fathers, papal encyclicals, and many other authoritative ecclesiastical documents. Having reached his conclusions, he laid them open to the public scrutiny and analysis of all men, but especially his scientific peers. He claimed no special privilege for them. He did not ask for them immunity from scientific criticism. He did not demand that their competitors should be suppressed and destroyed. All that he asked was what every scientist in every field asks for his findings: that they should be considered on their merits, in the spirit of scientific impartiality, of sportsmanlike fair play, without handicaps, without fouling.

This apparently the ecclesiastical interests for which Manning, McGeehan, and Goldstein speak do not find it safe to do. According to many, Mr. Manning's church was conceived in what Mr. McGeehan's church regards as the adultery of Henry VIII. The cults of these churches are peculiarly sensitive on sexual questions, and postulate certain mysteries of sex which will not bear scientific inquiry. Such dogmas as the Virgin Birth of Christ and the Immaculate Conception of the Virgin are necessarily taboo to what is usually meant by study and analysis, and the suppression spreads from these supernatural phenomena of sex to the natural ones. It is obvious that a candid, scientific treatment of the natural ones might lead to scrutiny of the supernatural ones with ecclesiastically undesirable results. Thus it is to the advantage of churchmen if people do not "scrutinize the depths of the mysteries of God but venerate them devoutly and humbly," as the encyclical *Pascendi Gregis* says. Consequently, studies such as those of Havelock Ellis on the psychology of sex, Westermarck and Letourneaux on human marriage, Henry Lea on sacerdotal celibacy, or Bertrand Russell on marriage and morals, become anathema to certain types of churchmen. In the case of Rus-

[43]

sell, the rights and powers of an appointive body are invaded, his source of livelihood is cut off, his character is libeled, and his opinions are described as sure to "aid and abet or encourage any course of conduct tending to a violation of the penal law." This is done ostensibly in defense of "morality," on an *ipse dixit* of a Catholic judge, without a shred of evidence, and without a hearing of the person thus libeled.

Now in scientific terms it is just as false that the opinions of Bertrand Russell on sexual behavior make for immorality as that the dogmas of the Catholic and Anglican churches make for morality. On the contrary, the testimony of past and present pupils of Bertrand Russell tends to show that his opinions do not make for immorality, while there is no testimony whatsoever that they do. And the data of educators, psychologists, and criminologists show that there is a high correlation between delinquency, crime, and churchly affiliation.

"Most criminals," writes Professor Carl Murchison, "belong to some church and frankly admit the fact. The big majority attend church services every Sunday morning in the Maryland Pen. . . . 14.3% are frankly agnostic. The criminal is religious, the vast majority belonging to some established religious denomination." [11] And Professor William C. Bagley writes:

The states and sections of our country where religious "fundamentalism" shows the fewest signs of "collapse" are the states and sections which have the heaviest ratios of the most serious crime (homicide) and which, in proportion to their population, have produced the greatest number of criminals. And among the states that have the lowest ratios of serious crime and apparently produce the fewest criminals in proportion to their population

[11] *Criminal Intelligence*, Worcester, 1926, p. 144.

[44]

are certain states in which a more liberal spirit unquestionably prevails.[12]

William Healy and Augusta Bronner studied 1636 delinquents before the Chicago Juvenile Court in 1910, and found that 90% of them were of religious background (56% of the total being Roman Catholics) and less than one-tenth of one per cent definitely of no religion.[13] For the State of Massachusetts they gave the following figures:

Religion	Reformatory Population	General Population
Roman Catholic	66.3	66.4
Protestant	28.6	25.2
Jewish	3.9	6.7
Other	1.2	1.7

In *The Individual Delinquent,* Dr. Healy declares:

It is quite evident that formal religious training has not prevented delinquency in many of our cases, when other strong personal or environmental conditions were not, as such, squarely met. Participation in religious education and religious communication has been quite general among our offenders, but of course the answer given by pastors of all congregations is that these have had the word, but not caught the spirit. Occasionally in certain unstable types there is a tendency to religious emotionalism and antisocial conduct at the same time. It is curious that in not over a dozen cases have we heard expressions of formed irreligious opinions . . . certain it is that, through not taking into account these other backgrounds of delinquency, such religious experience as most of our offenders have had has not proved thus sustaining. Many a parish would be bettered if the fundamental sources of misconduct were studied, enumerated, and treated in a scientific spirit.[14]

[12] *Education, Crime and Social Progress,* New York, 1931, p. 43.
[13] *Delinquents and Criminals,* New York, 1926.
[14] Boston, 1924, pp. 151-2.

The Professor of Neuropathology at New York Post-Graduate Medical School and Director of the New York Children's Court Clinic, Max G. Schlapp, and his associate Edward H. Smith declare:

The veriest amateur at disputation may confute the whole argument with the common observation that religious persons, not excepting priests and teachers of all sects and of the highest position, have in all times and upon innumerable occasions been guilty of the grossest crimes . . . if more evidence were needed to invalidate the claims of these old theorists it might readily be found in the tables of two generations of statisticians who have all concluded that the ratio of convicts without religious training and religious adhesions is about one-tenth of one per cent. The percentage of atheism is certainly not lower among the honest and unconfined, so we may dismiss the whole pretension of the spiritualists with a smile of incredulity.[15]

The testimony is similar when it comes to sex-offenses. William T. Root, Jr., Professor of Educational Psychology, University of Pittsburgh, Trustee of the Western Penitentiary of Pennsylvania,[16] wrote:

. . . the most perfect cases of sordid sex-offense and intense emotional religious sincerity are to be found among those imprisoned for sex-offenses.

He printed the following table:

	Protestant	Roman Catholic	Jewish	Indifferent (in per cents)
Predatory Crime	23	19.5	.6	9.3
Homicide	9.2	14.8	..	2.9
Sexual Crime	4.3	4.7	..	1.9 [17]

[15] *The New Criminology*, New York, 1928, pp. 56–7.
[16] *A Psychological and Educational Survey of 1916 Prisoners in the Western Penitentiary of Pennsylvania*, p. 192.
[17] Carl Murchison wrote: "The Methodists and the Catholics comprise

[46]

It is significant that research in Holland reveals similar findings. "Statistics," wrote Dr. W. A. Bonger, Professor of Criminology and Sociology at the University of Amsterdam, "leave no loophole for misunderstanding: criminality among irreligious persons is usually the lowest on the list." [18]

Delinquency of children in the United States shows corresponding ratios. According to the *Illinois Crime Survey*,[19] between 1900 and 1926 such delinquency among Jews ranged from 1.7% to 8.3%, among Protestants from 26.1% to 48.2%, among Catholics from 48% to 63.9%. Judge Cleland of Chicago is cited by C. V. Dunn [20] as saying that

---

approximately 50% of the prison population but commit more than 85% of the sex-crimes."

[18] *Introduction to Criminology*, London, 1936, p. 132. Bonger compiled the following table, based on government figures in a city primarily Protestant (*ibid.*, pp. 129 *et seq.*): Sentenced per 100,000 in Amsterdam, 1923–27, for crimes against morals: non-denominational 2.9; Jewish 2.12; Protestant 3.8; Catholic 5.3. For all crimes: non-denominational 39; Jewish 48.8; Protestant 50.6; Roman Catholic 61.8. Sex-crimes per 100,000, Holland, 1901–09: non-denominational 1.6; Jewish 4.1; Protestant 5.1; Roman Catholic 7.1. In 126,000 cases of crime in Holland between 1901 and 1909, he found for every 100 non-denominationals, 252 Jews, 366 Protestants, and 494 Roman Catholics.

According to G. H. Feber (*Die Criminaliteit der Katholicken in Nederland*, Maaseik, 1933), sex-crimes committed in Holland between 1901–1909 by persons over ten years of age show the following ratios to religions: Jews 4.1 per 100,000; Protestants 5.1; Roman Catholics 7.1. Persons of no religion yielded a ratio of only 1.6 per 100,000. The Jews, 2% of the population, had only 0.7% of such crimes; the Catholics, 35% of the population, provided 40.3% of such crimes; the Protestants, 59% of the population, provided 58.3 % of the sex crimes. S. H. Phillips (*Het Passioneele Misdrijt in Nederland*, Amsterdam, 1938) gives the figures for the years 1929–30. The Catholics, with 35.1% of the population, give 49.18% of the sex-crimes; the Protestants, with 47% of the population, give 45.9% of the sex-crimes; the Jews, with 1.5% of the population, give 0.55% of the sex-crimes.

[19] C. R. Shaw and E. D. Myers, "The Juvenile Delinquent," *Illinois Crime Survey*, Chicago, 1929, p. 669.

[20] "The Church and Crime in the United States," *Annals of the American Academy of Political and Social Science*, Philadelphia, 1926, p. 206.

[47]

out of 1000 prisoners before him 49.6% were Catholics, 48% Protestants, 1.5% Jews. Dunn's tables show that of 32,834 convicts in State prisons 49.3% were Protestant, 22.5% Roman Catholic, and the remainder divided among the Mormons, Jews, and innumerable other religious sects in the United States.[21]

This would make it appear that crime and delinquency are directly proportional to the intransigent dogmatism of theological and moral instruction. Ecclesiastical prohibition of contraception, of divorce, ecclesiastical handling of sex irregularities that psychologists, physicians, and educators understand far better than churchmen, correlate positively with the criminal record in these matters. Even before Hitler illegitimacy was higher in such countries as Bavaria, Austria, Poland, and Portugal than in religiously free countries. It is true that Ireland reports a low percentage of illegitimate births. But that may have something to do with the practice of transporting unmarried pregnant girls to Liverpool, Glasgow, and elsewhere before their babies are born.[22]

As for adultery, it seems to be a matter of ecclesiastical latitude. To priests of the Roman Catholic cultus any form of wedlock other than Roman Catholic is the same as no wedlock at all; a duly consecrated marriage of Catholics binds a couple until death, and divorce is forbidden, regardless of how disastrous the wedded bliss may be. If there is an unsanctioned divorce, remarriage after divorce is adultery. The substitute for divorce is ecclesiastical annulment, which makes marriage the same as if it had not taken place. But annulments are beyond the reach of the Catholic

[21] *Ibid.*, p. 206 ff.
[22] *Cf.* C. J. Cadoux, *Catholicism and Christianity*, New York, 1929, p. 625.

poor. As for marriages between Catholics and Protestants, they are held to be mere concubinage by the Catholic Church and therefore are not valid and do not require any pronouncement of the Roman Rota to annul them. In such cases the priest advises civil divorce, which leaves the Catholic party free to marry again without any action on the part of the Church.

Mixed marriages, of course, may be allowed after special dispensation (in this country), provided conditions are agreed to and signed and the marriage is performed only by a Catholic priest. A law of 1932, however, provides that such marriages (in some mysterious way) become invalid if the parties do not live up to their agreements after a number of years—education of the children as Catholics, for instance.

Such dispensations, however, are not allowed in many countries. The Province of Quebec, in Canada, is such a country, and if a Catholic marry a Protestant there before a Protestant minister, the civil court will annul the marriage.

That the Protestant churches are more generous in these matters is an old story. They have a low opinion of annulments, which only "break up homes and unfortunately add a stigma of shame to the marriage which has been annulled." [23]

Concerning "adultery," then, there seems to be, among the infallible sex-policemen of the Christian churches, some disagreement as to when it exists and when it does not exist. From the Catholic point of view, Bishop Manning might be said to believe in adultery. According to many a Prot-

---

[23] *Report of the Commission on Marriage and the Home*, Federal Churches of Christ in America. The Commissioners were Bishop Henry W. George Tucker, Episcopalian; James G. Cannon, Jr., Methodist; former Attorney General Geo. W. Wickersham, Mrs. John D. Rockefeller, Jr.

estant the Catholics create adultery by a canonical fiction where it does not exist. Different sects will give the seventh commandment different meanings, each as infallible as the other and each immune from examination on its merits.

VI

It is out of this sort of warfare of absolutes that the Protestant churches have come to the idea of toleration and the rule of *Live and Let Live,* which was in Roger Williams's mind when he declared:

It is the will and command of God, that . . . a permission of the most Paganish, Jewish, Turkish, or Antichristian consciences and worships be granted to all men in all Nations.

It is out of such present confrontations that Catholic Mr. Justice Murphy came to his conclusion that:

We need to be reminded that there is no hope in any program or philosophy which levels the finger of blame at a single group and seeks to bring peace and security by purging or suppressing that group.[24]

It is through such confrontations of alternatives that the liberated intelligence came at last to its faith in the method of intellectual freedom which we call science. Without the rule of live and let live in religion, without the chance of new and different ways of life and thought to try themselves out on their merits in science, history would be dead repetition of the past, progress would be unthinkable, growth impossible. If, as is argued, the younger generation should merely repeat without scrutiny, without challenge, without due consideration of alternatives, what their elders already know and believe, education would be turned into

---

[24] *New York Times,* March 2, 1940.

a costly and futile farce. If this doctrine had been successfully enforced in Judea, Jesus could never have taught or Christianity arisen; if it had been successfully applied to Copernicus, Galileo, Kepler, and Descartes, the world would have been without the sciences of nature of which it boasts. All variations, all new thoughts and inventions have, in the nature of things, a hard time getting a hearing. They appear, naturally, as the ideas of a minority, and it is of the essence of democracy that the right of any minority to equality under the law shall be safeguarded by the majority. The more the idea diverges from the idea of the majority, the more it requires the guarantee of the majority for the welfare of the majority, that it shall have an opportunity to make good on its merits, without fear and without favor.

In a democracy the educational establishments are where this opportunity is properly provided. In the schools and colleges, the new idea can be studied freely, and with a minimum of social risk and a maximum of social advantage. It can be scrutinized closely, freely compared with its alternatives, and judged impartially without that clash of vested practical interests which occurs in the extra-mural world. It is to just such scrutiny, comparison, and judgment that Bertrand Russell offered his observations and judgments on sexways. And from this simple, open, unafraid scientific attitude McGeehan's Catholic logic deduces that he was *urging* people to violate a State statute which makes cohabitation with girls under eighteen years of age a felony. The logic is the more significant in the light of the fact that Goldstein had admitted that Russell had said that his conclusions regarding sexual morality were not likely to be acceptable until long after everybody now past middle age was dead.

[5 1]

Was it not persecution of this order that Mr. Justice Holmes had in mind when he wrote:

But when men have realized that time has upset many fighting faiths, they may come to believe even more than they believe the very foundations of their own conduct that the ultimate good desired is better reached by free trade in ideas—that the best test of truth is the power of thought to get itself accepted in the competition of the market; and that truth is the only ground upon which their wishes safely can be carried out. That, at any rate, is the theory of our Constitution.

It is an experiment as all life is an experiment. Every year, if not every day, we have to wager our salvation upon some prophecy based upon imperfect knowledge.

While that experiment is part of our system I think that we should be eternally vigilant against attempts to check the expression of opinions that we loathe and believe fraught with death, unless they so imminently threaten immediate interference with the lawful and pressing purposes of the law that an immediate check is required to save the country.

Was it not to protect the consciences of free men and women from persecution of this order that Thomas Jefferson wrote into the Resolution of the Bill of Rights which Virginia adopted in 1785:

To suffer the civil magistrate to intrude his power in the field of opinion, or to restrain the profession or propagation of principles on *the supposition of their ill tendency*, is a dangerous fallacy, which at once destroys all liberty, because he, being of course the judge of that tendency, will make his opinions the rule of judgment, and approve or condemn the sentiments of others only as they square with or differ from his own. It is time enough for the rightful purpose of Civil Government for its officers to interfere *when principles break out into overt acts* against peace and good order.

[5 2]

This is the Americanism of the foremost teacher of American democracy among the Founding Fathers and of those who share his democratic faith. Does the "Russell case" conceal an ecclesiastical-political assault on this Americanism?

SOCIAL REALITIES
VERSUS
POLICE COURT FICTIONS

By John Dewey

Social Realities *versus*
Police Court Fictions

IN 1929 there was published in New York City a book
dealing with the social and personal ethics of the family
from the conjugal and familial points of view, the latter
having to do especially with the interests of children but
also including economic aspects of the family as a household unit. The public reception of the book at the time is
fairly represented by the following extracts from reviews
in New York City papers. By one critic the author is said to
"deal most competently and completely with practically
every ramification of sex and sex-life that occurs in modern
sociology and psychology"; the critic referred specifically
to the book's "dignified pages." Another reviewer flatly said
of the book that it was "the most humane and persuasive
volume in the recent books on marriage," while a third one
said that the book "is valuable for being at once fundamental
and clear, unbiased and persuasive," that the author is writing "as a humanist, defending the happiness of man against
many moral prejudices."

Several years before the appearance of the book in question, a writer of the Roman Catholic persuasion had written
in the *Catholic World* concerning the author, whose reputation was already well established, as "a religious atheist."

Although, of course, the Catholic writer rejected the "religious atheist's" views, he said of him: "He is a man of high intellectual achievement, and of undoubted honesty of purpose"; "one of our clearest and most penetrating thinkers, and, whatever our judgment of his ideals, undoubtedly an idealist." In another place this Catholic writer said, in a passage directly relevant to the theme of the later work of the author: "In the Chapter on 'Marriage' in *Principles of Social Reconstruction* we read: 'As religion dominated the old form of marriage, so religion must dominate the new.' It is good that Mr. Russell should see so clearly that no legal rules or permissions can, by themselves, solve the problems of sex-relationship, that these are soluble by religion alone." Regarding the general position taken by the author whom the Catholic writer was discussing, the latter quotes the following passage as typical: "If life is to be fully human, it must serve some end which seems, in some sense, outside human life; some end which is impersonal and above mankind, such as God or truth or beauty," and after citing other passages says: "Such is the religious witness of Mr. Russell, valuable surely as the witness borne by one of the keenest intellects to which naturalism can appeal for support."

Eleven years after the appearance of the book of which reviewers spoke so highly in 1929, its author was characterized by a lawyer, representing a client in an alleged court of justice, as "lecherous, salacious, libidinous, lustful, venerous, erotomaniac, aphrodisiac, atheistic, irreverent, narrow-minded, untruthful, and bereft of moral fiber . . . he is a sophist; practices sophism; by cunning contrivances, tricks, and devices, and by mere quibbling he puts forth fallacious arguments . . . all his alleged doctrines which he calls philosophy are just cheap, tawdry, worn out, patched up fetishes and propositions, devises [*sic*] for misleading the people."

The judge who passed upon the case in court said that the contention that "immoral and salacious doctrines" were taught in the books written by the author in question was amply sustained; that they are full of "filth"; that the principle of "academic freedom was being used as a cloak to promote the popularization in the minds of adolescents of acts forbidden by the penal law"; that the writer was a man whose life and teachings run counter to the doctrines "which have been held sacred by all Americans, preserved by the Constitution of the United States and of the several States, defended by the blood of its citizens"; that the man in question "teaches and practices immorality and . . . encourages and avows violation of the penal law of the State of New York."

It is no secret to the reader that the book thus denounced is *Marriage and Morals* and that the author thus excoriated is Bertrand Russell.

The full story is told elsewhere in the present volume, and the bearing of the decision upon the well-being of schools, public and private, is competently discussed. These matters are outside the scope of my particular contribution to this book. I shall say nothing of the extensive acquaintance of the lawyer with the vocabulary of obscenity or of the fact that the "justice" who heard the case indulged in language which if uttered where it did not have the protection of judicial position would have been outright libelous, although he also took advantage of the same judicial position to deny Mr. Russell a chance to appear and to exercise the ordinary right of self-defense. I gladly leave these men, lawyer and judge, to the kind of immortality in the annals of history they have won for themselves.

I shall not even raise a question that is of great social importance: How and why is it that in eleven short years there has been such a growth of intolerance and bigotry? My part in this volume of record and protest is to point out the immense difference between the realities of the case in what Mr. Russell actually said about the past, present, and possible ethics of marriage and sex, and the opinion, involving unbridled misrepresentations, expressed by attorney and Court. The opinion of the Court was allowed to pass, with no opportunity for Mr. Russell to obtain a hearing, and his right of appeal to a higher court was denied on a technicality which is irrelevant to the merits of the case. As Americans we can only blush with shame for this scar on our repute for fair play.

But, it may be asked, whatever be said about the Court's interpretation, are not the passages cited by it actually found in the book? They are, and yet, by adopting the method employed by the Court, I could show that Mr. Russell's opinions are in substantial harmony with the best traditional views on the topics discussed. For the method was the cheap device of quoting passages without reference to their context and without reference to the purpose of the arguments in which they appear.

For example, the following passages are infinitely more representative of the purpose of the discussion and of the question of decency *versus* filth than are the extracts arbitrarily selected by the Court—or by whoever wrote its decision: "Marriage is something more serious than the pleasure of two people in each other's company; it is an institution which, through the fact that it gives rise to children, forms part of the intimate texture of society and has an importance extending far beyond the personal feelings of the husband and wife." "I believe marriage to be the best and most im-

[60]

portant relation that can exist between two human beings." "Custom should be against divorce except in somewhat extreme cases."

So much for marriage. As for sex and the sexual act, I quote the following passages: "A comprehensive sexual ethic cannot regard sex merely as a natural hunger. Sex is connected with some of the greatest goods in human life, lyric love, happiness in marriage, and art." "Love increases in value in proportion as more of the personalities of the people concerned enters into the relation." "I wish to repeat, as emphatically as I can, that an undue preoccupation with this topic [sex] is an evil." "One of the most dangerous of fallacies is the reduction of sex to the sexual act." "We regard it as wrong to steal food. . . . Restraints of a similar kind are essential where sex is concerned, but in this case they are more complex and involve much more self-control." Mr. Russell criticizes novelists who "view sex-intercourse merely as a physiological outlet"; "love," he holds, "has its own ideals and its own intrinsic moral standards."

I could quote many other passages of the same tenor. If, however, they were permitted to stand alone they would fail to do justice to the purpose and spirit of Mr. Russell's book. While the passages are, as I have said, representative, and Justice McGeehan's extracts are misrepresentative, they occur in the course of a criticism of the traditional and conventional ethic of sex and of marriage. It is this ethic, according to Mr. Russell, which fails to conform to the ideal character of love, and which tends to degrade the sex-act to something inherently unworthy and, even according to the views of St. Paul and many of the Church fathers, intrinsically indecent; the prevalence of this ethic being the main cause of taboos on proper instruction of

[61]

the young. Indeed, the sole charitable opinion that can be formed, by stretching charity to the utmost, of Justice McGeehan is that he himself, because of his education and environment, shares those views so fully that he regards *any* discussion of sexual matters as intrinsically indecent.

Mr. Russell's book is, then, an outright criticism of the traditional views of sex and marriage, views which have profoundly influenced law and public opinion. The book is a plea for views, for legal institutions, for social customs, and for public opinion, which will, in Mr. Russell's considered judgment, represent a more humane ethic and better serve the general welfare of society. Mr. Russell does not regard any position he takes as beyond criticism. But he would wish the criticism to be made on the same grounds of rational examination, free from superstitious traditions, and in the light of the moral standard of general well-being and happiness, upon which he rests his own views. He was not unaware of the interpretation that would be put upon his views by men of the mental and moral habits of the justice, several clerics, and such outstanding authorities as Mr. George Harvey of Queens and various lodges of the Ancient Order of Hibernians; for in his book he said: "The writer who deals with a sexual theme is always in danger of being accused, by those who think that such themes should not be mentioned, of an undue obsession with his subject. It is thought he would not risk the censure of prudish and prurient persons unless his interest in the subject were out of all proportion to its importance. . . . I am quite in agreement with the Church in thinking that obsession with sexual topics is an evil, but I am not in agreement with the Church as to the best methods of avoiding this evil."

I am aware that people who are sincere and in general

high-minded, have been so deeply influenced by the taboos which surrounded the subject of sex in their early education that many of them, although they had not read Mr. Russell's book, were willing to take the outcry against the book and its author for what it pretended to be. But those who *are* genuinely sincere and high-minded will be willing, even if they retain their own traditional views, to admit that a man who is a scholar and who is deeply concerned for social values may hold other views than their own, and may hold them on definite moral grounds. If they believe in the value of free intelligence and inquiry, they will concede to others the right of public examination and discussion, provided those are conducted in a way that is intellectually competent and morally serious.

This brings me to the important point in insistence on social realities against court-room fictions, namely, the ethic actually held by Mr. Russell. What is this ethic? His own statement is explicit. "Sex morality has to be derived from certain general principles, as to which there is perhaps a fairly wide measure of agreement, in spite of the wide disagreement as to the consequence to be drawn from them. The first thing to be secured is that there should be as much as possible of that deep, serious love between man and woman which embraces the whole personality of both and leads to a fusion by which each is enriched and enhanced. . . . The second thing of importance is that there should be adequate care of children, physical and psychological." It may be doubted whether the original complainant, Mrs. Kay, her attorney, Mr. Goldstein, or the justice, Mr. McGeehan, can find (upon the unlikely supposition that they ever read the book) anything "lecherous, salacious, libidinous, etc., etc." in this passage, expert as they assume to be in such matters. The following passage rep-

[63]

resents the contrast Mr. Russell finds existing between the conclusions he draws from these principles and those drawn from views more widely held: "The doctrine that there is something sinful about sex is one which has done untold harm to individual character—a harm beginning in early childhood and continuing through life. By keeping sex-love in a prison, conventional morality has done much to imprison all other forms of friendly feeling, and to make men less generous, less kindly, more self-assertive, and more cruel. Whatever sexual ethic may come to be ultimately accepted must be free from superstition and must have recognizable and demonstrable grounds in its favor." "Sex," says Russell, "cannot dispense with an ethic, any more than business or sport or scientific research or any other branch of human activity. But it can dispense with an ethic based solely upon ancient prohibitions propounded by uneducated people in a society wholly unlike our own. In sex, as in economics and in politics, our ethic is still dominated by fears which modern discoveries have made irrational. . . . It is true that the transition from the old system to the new has its own difficulties, as all transitions have. . . . The morality which I should advocate does not consist simply of saying to grown-up people or adolescents: 'Follow your impulses and do as you like.' There has to be consistency in life; there has to be continuous effort directed to ends that are not immediately beneficial and not at every moment attractive; there has to be consideration for others; and there should be certain standards of rectitude. . . . It is impossible to judge a new morality fairly until it has been applied in early education." [1]

---

[1] I have quoted liberally because it is an incidental irony that this book, so bitterly denounced, is no longer in print and cannot be bought through the regular channels of trade.

There is another point to be taken into consideration when passing judgment upon the book. It certainly is essential that the tone and temper of the discussion should be in keeping with the underlying moral principles which are advocated, that it should be serious and dignified. In a book that in important matters goes contrary to current beliefs it is especially indispensable that the discussion be carried on with high seriousness as well as candor. No quotations of mine, short of citing the whole book, can be conclusive on this point. But anyone who with honest spirit has read the book as a whole, knows, and if he be honest will be ready to testify —regardless of whether he agrees with its argument or does not agree—that the book is addressed to adults who are supposed (perhaps overgenerously) to have, themselves, a serious moral interest in the subject and to be capable of drawing their conclusions on the basis of facts and reasonable arguments. The chapters of the book consist of anthropological, historical, sociological, and psychological data, assembled from recognized authorities in these fields. That the book is addressed to adolescents—such as would be taught in a college class—is a falsehood; it is equally false that if it were read by adolescents (as it might well be) it would be found to advocate looseness of conduct, judged even by conventional standards, on their part. What it advocates, consistently and without exception, is a change in public opinion which will make possible a sexual ethic and moral habits, personal and social, which, in the opinion of Mr. Russell, are of a higher order than those which now exist. It is impossible to characterize any other opinion of the book, even though it be put forth in an alleged court of justice, as anything except a deliberate misrepresentation.

I come now to the specific points upon which the Court based its condemnation of Mr. Russell and gave as reasons for nullifying his appointment by the Board of Higher Education. Mr. Russell made some remarks on the evils of methods that are in vogue of dealing with the practice of masturbation. The remarks are commonplaces of competent medical discussion. The really important matter in this connection is not the remarks of Mr. Russell, which are supported by experience and, as I have said, by practically universal medical opinion. The really important matter is the fact that the method used by the Court gives convincing evidence of the latter's intent to make out a case without reference to the state of fact. For the Court's intent is to place Mr. Russell in the light of advising the practice of masturbation. Consequently, he omits a passage in which Mr. Russell explicitly recommends the use, in the endeavor to check it, of procedures other than direct prohibition which is accompanied by threats of dire consequences (insanity, etc.). These other procedures, if adopted, would tend to reduce the likelihood that children will indulge in the practice. Of course, had this passage been quoted, it would of itself have been enough to disprove the contention that Mr. Russell was promoting and sponsoring the practice of masturbation.

Extracts from what Mr. Russell has written on the topic of nudity in children and adults are also brought forward as a ground for condemning him as a man of such immoral character that he ought not to be permitted to teach youth. Mr. Russell advanced the view that "It is good for children to see each other and their parents naked, *whenever it so happens naturally*. No fuss should be made either way." This view appears monstrous to Justice McGeehan, and he quoted the passage as a proof that Mr. Russell's appointment is in effect an establishment of a "chair of indecency." It is typical of McGeehan's judicial processes that he makes

[66]

no reference to the reasons given by Russell for coming to this conclusion: that the opposite practice evokes "the sense that there is mystery, and having that sense they [the children] will become prurient and indecent." This belief is one item of Mr. Russell's indictment of conventional ideas and practices. For the conventions have enveloped sex in an atmosphere of mystery and secrecy, and by so doing have done very much to create and to foster the very indecencies which are nominally deplored. Quite independently of anything Mr. Russell ever said on the subject, hundreds and hundreds of intelligent and honorable parents in our country have reached a similar conclusion as a result of their own experience. In what concerns nudity and children, the attitude commended by Mr. Russell has long been standard.

As to adults, Mr. Russell writes: "There are many important grounds of health in favor of nudity in *suitable circumstances* such as out of doors in sunny weather." Utterance of this hygienic commonplace is perhaps the ground for the statement of the attorney purporting to speak for Mrs. Kay that Mr. Russell once personally conducted a nudist colony; apparently, no interpretation of what Mr. Russell has said and done was too absurd or too arbitrary to keep Mr. Goldstein from perpetrating it. The bathing costumes now in vogue on most beaches in the country would certainly once have caused the arrest of people wearing them; if such bathing-suit cases had ever come before Justice McGeehan one can infer from his handling of the point in the matter of Mr. Russell's appointment with what relish and gusto he would have dealt with them. It is also true that the change in the public attitude is evidence for Mr. Russell's contention that much of the sense of indecency which has been attached to certain customs disappears when the customs in question change.

[67]

The matters just mentioned fall within the scope of the things which Justice McGeehan said gave him no ground for interference. For it is one of the extraordinary features of the extraordinary opinion of the Court that more than half of it is an attack upon Mr. Russell's views and conduct in matters which, by the justice's own admission, were quite out of his jurisdiction. In his own words, "As to such conduct, this court is powerless to act because of the power conferred by law on the Board of Higher Education." The space given to abuse of Mr. Russell in matters which according to the Court's own statement were none of its judicial business is enough by itself alone to prove the existence of a concealed animus back of the whole affair.

The opinion of the Court is so confused and so mixes up the things regarding which it said it had no power to act with the matters in which it assumed it had power to nullify the action of the Board of Higher Education, that it is not easy to tell, on the ground of what Justice McGeehan states, just what views of Mr. Russell tended in the Court's opinion to "aid, abet, encourage" violations of the penal code, so that the Board had acted "to sponsor or encourage violations of the penal law." For the justice quotes, with his usual relish, provisions of the penal code against abduction and rape, which even he did not and could not accuse Mr. Russell of advising and recommending. The probability, however, is that the things he makes the basis of his claim to jurisdiction are Mr. Russell's views on extra-marital relations of husband and wife; on sexual relations between young men and young women, especially university students, before marriage; and on homosexuality. Aside from details of the Court's treatment of these points, there is one feature which marks everything that the Court said: nowhere does His Honor allude to the reasons that Mr. Russell advanced for putting forth his

[68]

particular views, and everywhere he treats Mr. Russell's argument in favor of a change in public opinion which will finally result in a change of custom and law as if it were a recommendation to people to engage in practices that are contrary both to traditional opinions and to the law as it now stands.

I begin with the question of homosexuality. In *Marriage and Morals* Mr. Russell discusses the inadvisability of laws regulating obscenity. He argues that no such law can be so drawn that it may not be used to suppress the public discussion and the literary productions that should have the right to appear. In the course of this argument Mr. Russell calls attention to the fact that, according to English law, not only is "any treatment of homosexuality in fiction illegal" but also that "it would be very difficult to present any argument for a change in the law which would not itself be illegal on the ground of obscenity." According to English law, "homosexuality between men but not between women is illegal," so that, Mr. Russell remarks, the effect of the law on obscenity has been to promote retention on the statute books of a law which "every person who has taken the trouble to study the matter knows is an effect of a barbarous and ignorant superstition." Justice McGeehan does not cite this passage, possibly because the passage itself, even if his practice of consistent ignoring of context had been dropped, made it clear that change in existing law was the aim of the discussion. His Honor does quote the following passage from an earlier book of Mr. Russell's, *Education and the Modern World:* "It is possible that homosexual relations with other boys would not be very harmful if they were tolerated, but even then there is danger lest they should interfere with the growth of a normal sexual life later on." This hypothetical statement of a *possibility,* accompanied as it is with an argument *against* rather than *for* the practice, becomes in the Court's opinion advocacy of a "damnable felony." Just what the honorable judge would say about physicians who have written much more unguardedly than has Mr. Russell in case their writings came before him may be left to the imagination. I hope that quotation of the following sentence from *A Survey of Child Psychiatry* written by Dr. J. R. Rees (1939) will not get its author into trouble or be interpreted as an endorsement by me of homosexuality among boys. "Homosexuality may be regarded as a normal phase of development in both sexes. . . . Provided the general emotional situation of the child is as it should be, there will be a natural development through this phase on to heterosexuality." [2]

Mr. Russell's views upon the subjects of sexual relations between unmarried youth of opposite sexes and in certain cases upon extra-marital relations on the part of husband and wife are undoubtedly shocking to upholders of the conventional moral code. They are also the views most likely to arouse dissent of a certain amount and kind among persons whose ideas on the standpoint from which sexual matters and marriage should be considered are similar to those of Mr. Russell. What is at issue, with respect to Justice McGeehan's method of treatment and his characterizations of Mr. Russell (which, I repeat, would be libelous if their author could not shelter himself behind the privilege of a court), is not the correctness or the wisdom of Mr. Russell's particular views. What is at issue is the wisdom or

---

[2] In fairness to the author, it should be noted that "homosexuality" is used in a very wide sense by members of the Freudian school. It covers "emotional interest in persons of the same sex" as against such interest in persons of the other sex, and includes more than commission of overt acts of the type to which the word "sexual" is usually limited outside of psychiatric circles.

unwisdom of public discussion of sex and marriage when these topics are approached in a scientific manner and with serious, ethical interest. Anyone who reads Mr. Russell's complete text in a frame of mind at all reasonable will find that he states his views, be they wise or unwise, in a way that well satisfies both of these conditions. Such a reader will note that Mr. Russell is definitely concerned with moral evils in customs which do undeniably exist already alike among unmarried youth and married adults. Such a reader will note that it is in the interest of a change in public opinion, custom, and in legal rules that Mr. Russell advocates an alternative ethic.[3]

According to an account of an interview with Mr. Russell published recently in a newspaper, he himself has found reason, in one important matter, for modifying views earlier expressed. He now thinks divorce more often preferable to trying to patch up an unsatisfactory marriage. Changes such as this are an indication of his general scientific method and moral seriousness. They tie up with the fact that nowhere in his writings is there any claim that the views expressed are final or intended for any purpose other than the ultimate promotion, by means of scientific discussion, of a higher type of ethic than now exists.

Other persons have written in this volume about the legal aspects of the case and about its connection with educational policies. I have said what I have to say in the con-

---

[3] The disingenuousness of the Court is on the surface in the case of what is said about "companionate marriage." For in this matter it is obvious on its face that the discussion concerns change in existing law, and that the change is argued for on the precise ground that the effect of legalized "companionate" marriage would be to reduce casual, surreptitious sexual relations among youth, and to promote relations prompted by serious and perhaps enduring affection in contrast with the strength of mere sexual desire now so common in actual practice among youth of all sects.

viction that, quite apart from the baleful consequence of the Court's decision in respect to school and education, this decision is to be condemned on two other grounds. One of them is the flagrant injustice done a gentleman and a scholar. Probably not one-tenth of one per cent of members of the various organizations that rushed to attack Mr. Russell's supposed views and to support Justice McGeehan ever read anything of Mr. Russell's save perhaps the passages extracted (or extorted) by the justice in his opinion and repeated in a gloating press. Hundreds, and perhaps thousands, of other persons who knew nothing of what Mr. Russell actually teaches were thus led to look upon him with moral suspicion and aversion. In these circumstances, I regard it as a personal privilege to express publicly my deep conviction of the wrong done Mr. Russell.

The other reason for my particular contribution to this volume is more serious, and would be regarded as such, I am sure, by Mr. Russell himself. Wicked as is the personal injustice which has been done him under cover of what purported to be judicial action, it is, as he himself declared, relatively insignificant beside the question whether the issues and problems of social morals, in fields where conventional taboos are very strong, are or are not to be publicly discussed by scientifically competent persons. Many people believe that present practices and customs are morally much lower than they need be and that one cause of this lowness is the taboos upon discussion of sexual matters, taboos which preclude proper instruction of the young with respect to sex. Such people may be deterred from saying and doing what they might (and should) do toward the creation of a higher condition of moral practice, because they are not willing to undergo the unrestrained abuse heaped

[7 2]

upon Mr. Russell. Especially are they held back when they learn that even the common, ordinary right to appear in their own defense is likely to be denied them. The net effect of the McGeehan decision, thus, can only be to maintain the low standards which prevail in practice; to keep up the convention that if existing habits are not publicly discussed they do not exist. The decision serves, then, only to perpetuate the belief that no matter how undesirable are existing habits, they should not be mentioned publicly, since human nature is so constituted that nothing can be done—a belief I hold to be more current among "respectable" people than we like to admit. The action of Justice McGeehan was bad enough in its consequences. The evil was increased by the attitude of the Corporation Counsel in refusing to appeal the case, and by the complaisance of a "reform" Mayor who, after straining at Bertrand Russell, swallowed a Jimmy Walker.

It would seem as if all intelligent persons interested in a social ethic which is based upon social realities scientifically made known and which is directed to just and humane social ends could at least agree that darkness always attends suppression of the possibility of public discussion, and that the darkness, here as elsewhere, makes it easier for evil customs to endure and to flourish. I would not have legal measures censure even the mass of cheap sexuality presented on the stage and in public prints. But what is to be said of the state of a public opinion which delights in the former, yet is easily rallied to oppose serious intellectual discussion of sex and to revile those who act upon a belief that such discussion is a precondition of a better social ethic? The load of hypocrisy, conscious and unconscious, that is borne along on the shoulders of public opinion is one of the things most discouraging

[7 3]

to those who would like to keep their faith in the possibility of a more enlightened and more honest public morality.

The evocation, the promotion, and the solidification of hypocrisy because of the way in which the Russell appointment was treated is an event which by comparison makes the wisdom and unwisdom of particular changes advocated by Mr. Russell of no great moment. If they are unwise, surely public discussion, upon the basis of free inquiry and scientific knowledge employed by Mr. Russell, would lead to statement of and agreement upon wiser views. On the other hand, the action of the Court and of the institutional forces which promoted and supported its action tend to cut off discussion even on the grounds of reason and knowledge, although such discussion alone would be sure to uncover whatever mistakes there may be in Mr. Russell's proposals. The prospect of a better, a more sincere, and a more intelligent social morality, as well as of sound education in the school, has been blacked out.

The hopeful feature of the situation is the number and quality of scholars, scientific men, public-spirited citizens, and educators who have risen in defense of the scientific freedom for which Mr. Russell stands. I am privileged to have some part, however small, in this defense.

TRIAL BY ORDEAL, NEW STYLE

By Walton H. Hamilton

Trial by Ordeal, New Style*

T HE good old custom of trial by ordeal still endures.
But as judges, who have always been learned, have
become literate, it has changed its form. Fire, water, hot
irons have receded; the syllogism, the reference of instance
to category, the staccato of an unruly dialectic have come
into their places. In so verbal a ceremonial where a parade
of sequiturs separates premises from conclusion, there is
many a chance for a "therefore" to go astray; and the arbi-
ter who would keep a combat at law the instrument of justice must be wise in the vagrant ways of the mind. Great
jurists—Stone, Cardozo, Black, for example—admit the
difficulty of their task and confess their human frailty. They
practice an elusive art, keenly aware of the pitfalls into
which the would-be omniscient judge may fall: assumption
of the point to be proved, the trespass of the abstract rule on
the facts, the mask of logic worn by the undistributed middle, the use of colorful words to prod a balking reason, the
putting of the question in a way that will induce the answer
sought. For one who cries to the courts there is no escape
from a judgment which emerges from an exercise with fictions. But due process would seem to demand that he who
resorts to the law has the right to a proper ceremonial performed by a priest well versed in its mysteries.

---

* This essay, written for this volume, by permission of the editors and
publisher appeared in slightly modified form in the *Yale Law Journal*,
March 1941.—*Eds.*

Such a right to due process has been denied Bertrand Russell. If his equity in a chair at City College is to be resolved by legal law, he is entitled to a fair and honest bout. The challenge must come from a party entitled to make it; it must be entertained by a court of competent jurisdiction; judgment must emerge from the application of established norms to the distinctive circumstances of the instant case.

Yet here the protest has been taken by a person who can scarcely be accorded a legal interest in the matter; the court presents no convincing proof that it has warrant to hear the cause; the principles by which the facts are commuted into an adverse holding reside in no legal authority. The issue is entertained and resolved by a judge who is superbly unaware of the hazards indigenous to his calling. In an opinion of some five thousand words—half of which represent a labor of supererogation—the judge rises to every error which opportunity presents. Nasty names confer the human touch and a preconceived answer supplies the target for a wayward logic. Given the judge, the judgment could have been predicted—and that without reference to statute or precedent. But, even given the judge, no judicial analyst could have predicted the ideo-mosaic of syllogisms or the distinguished use of the word "therefore." In spite of his crimes against ignorance, Bertrand Russell deserved a bout at law under an umpire who could at least affect conformity with the great ceremonial.[1]

In a proper sequence of steps decorum observes the

---

[1] One wonders why the court's judgment does not, through its denial of a civil liberty, present a substantial Federal question which under the aegis of due process might be carried to the Supreme Court. That judicial scotching of such liberties may be constitutional ground for relief in Washington, see *American Federation of Labor v. Swing*, 9 *U. S. Law Week* 4192 (U. S. 1941); cf. *Milk Wagon Drivers Union v. Meadowmoor Dairies, Inc.*, 9 *U. S. Law Week* 4185 (U. S. 1941).

ritual. The faithful referee is eternally vigilant to confine the battle within the bounds of fair play. Lest there be taunts of Star Chamber, each round must be complete before the next is called. But Justice McGeehan, racing to uphold the victor's hand, telescoped the rounds and sped to judgment over murmurs from protagonist and defender alike.[2] The Justice sat as judge to hear motions, not to conduct trial.[3] Before him was only a motion—to dismiss an action against the Board of Higher Education. Without further ado, he reserved the motion, held trial, rendered judgment, and closed the case. Lost was the immemorial right to answer to charges filed; ignored were objections to irregularities of process. The urge against free thought left no time for the etiquette of stately adjudication.

Aside from the slurred-over proprieties, the Justice denies us landmarks by which to place the substance.[4] Jean Kay, who tilts against the Board of Education, is presumably a woman; and the newspapers—a void to the jurist and hearsay to me—report her to be a mother. But gentility in sex is not a passport to any legal arena; and even maternity in distress must present its cause of action. As to why the lady went tattling to the court, and as to why the jurist allowed himself to be diverted from cosmic matters, we know nothing. The opinion throws little light

---

[2] Jean Kay's attorney, when told to proceed with evidence in a motion hearing, balked at first. Counsel for the city subsequently objected to findings without benefit of answer or trial. Comment, "The Bertrand Russell Case: The History of a Litigation" (1940), 53 *Harvard Law Review* 1192.

[3] Rules of the Supreme Court, First Judicial District, New York County —Special Terms, Rule I authorized the term in which Justice McGeehan was sitting to hear motions, not to conduct trials.

[4] It is interesting to note that while the opinion makes frequent reference to judicial precedents in regard to minor matters, there is a total absence of citation of authority in what Justice McGeehan concedes to be the most important part of the opinion.

upon these initial—yet essential—matters. A casual word here and there implies—it does not say—that this is a taxpayer's suit, and a headnote which goes a little further than the text warrants seems to confirm. A taxpayer has a stake in his own return and if more is collected than is due, he has his case; but, even in so personal an affair, the rule is to pay first and sue for the refund. In any case, the courts have been grudging in allowing a taxpayer to challenge the use to which tax receipts are put.[5] Now and then one is allowed to plead that an expenditure which includes dollars he has paid does not serve a public purpose.[6] At best, a very dubious best, Jean Kay might be permitted to challenge an appropriation for public education, or perhaps to protest the squandering of the people's money on so esoteric a subject as philosophy. But it is difficult to vest her as a taxpayer with a legal interest in *who* is to have and to hold a chair of mathematics. And, however severely her conscience may chastise her into legal combat, her disguise as a taxpayer is perfectly transparent when she questions the moral character of a teacher.

In the sight of the judge, her cause is a crusade; it follows that she is entitled to whatever form of action is in stock. The law has provided her conscience with no appropriate action; its gross negligence does not lie at her door; she is driven to an improper remedy only for want of a proper one. But jurisdiction, even though the layman views it as hocus-pocus, is an institution of social significance. Through jurisdiction the courts close their doors to questions which can be better answered in some other

---

[5] *Massachusetts v. Mellon*, 262 U. S. 447 (1923).

[6] See *Campbell v. City of New York*, 244 N. Y. 317, 155 N. E. 628 (1927); *Hathaway v. Oneonta*, 148 Misc. 695, 266 N. Y. Supp. 237 (Sup. Ct. 1933); *Altschul v. Ludwig*, 216 N. Y. 459, 111 N. E. 216 (1916).

forum; through it they limit their discretion to matters which fall within the orbit of their special competence; through it they protect a going society against interference by persons who would affect their trifling interests with a legal concern.[7] If Jean Kay is in any way incommoded or distrained by the Russell appointment, it is not in her capacity of taxpayer; resort to the law promises to abate her assessment by not one cent. The newspapers have described her motive as solicitude lest the souls of her offspring be put in mortal jeopardy. If such be the case—the opinion seems to corroborate with circumstantial evidence—maternal concern has no need of resort to legal process. Bertrand Russell's courses were to have been elective, an offering for youths advanced enough in morality to forsake superstition. And, if the contagion were to spread to the whole climate of campus opinion, Jean Kay could send her young into the Bible Belt or even guard their innocence against any exposure to the higher learning.

But for a special *causa matris*—even where the mother makes up like a taxpayer—there is no statutory provision. Nor have judges, in the wisdom of their experience, seen fit to create so exposed a form of action. Mothers are an unstandardized lot; their urges run the spectrum of all the emotions. Their solicitude for their young presents a motley pattern; there is no unity in maternal beliefs as to which sort of words of teachers will incite immature youth to sin. If one would shield against honest utterance about the facts of life, another would tolerate no plain speech about business enterprise, and a third would refuse to condone any criticism of the national state. Among a people whose culture makes them severally parts of one another,

---

[7] Foster, "Jurisdiction" (1932), 8 *Encyclopaedia of the Social Sciences* 471.

morality cannot be an attribute of sex alone; the taint of ethics attaches to every personal relationship. There is not an aspect of life—race, religion, the arts, literature, finance, government, human nature—in which a critical attitude toward dominant belief could not be challenged as immoral. Nor is there any staircase rising from the profane to the secular by which indulgences may be allowed in venial matters and blasphemy outlawed in mortal ones. A brief two centuries ago an age which accepted the common whore as a shield for maidenly virtue rose in a great "moral storm" [8] to consign the theater to perdition. The nineteen-twenties found imbibition [9] as baleful, in law at least, as white-slavery or free love. In a section of our land where the folk are at home with the fundamentals, a

---

[8] While to the mind of Justice McGeehan morality is exclusively a matter of sex, the moral urge is unpurposive. The many directions in which it may be impelled have been well described by Mr. Justice Holmes, dissenting, in *Tyson v. Banton,* 273 U. S. 418, 446–7 (1927):

"The truth seems to me to be that, subject to compensation when compensation is due, the legislature may forbid or restrict any business when it has a sufficient force of public opinion behind it. Lotteries were thought useful adjuncts of the State a century or so ago; now they are believed to be immoral and they have been stopped. Wine has been thought good for man from the time of the Apostles until recent years. But when public opinion changed, it did not need the Eighteenth Amendment, notwithstanding the Fourteenth, to enable a State to say that the business should end. What has happened to lotteries and wine might happen to theaters in some moral storm of the future, not because theaters were devoted to a public use, but because people had come to think that way.

"But if we are to yield to fashionable conventions, it seems to me that theaters are as much devoted to public use as anything well can be. We have not that respect for art that is one of the glories of France. But to many people the superfluous is the necessary, and it seems to me that Government does not go beyond its sphere in attempting to make life livable for them. I am far from saying that I think this particular law a wise and rational provision. That is not my affair."

[9] Viewing the following instance in terms of 1941 highlights the ephemeral nature of a taboo: during prohibition a professor of philosophy at the University of Virginia was suspended from his office for one year because local police had discovered one bottle of whisky in his automobile.

[82]

statement that the world was not made in six days is far more outrageous than soft words about so polysyllabic a thing as homosexuality. Age, section, group, nation, culture —each has woven its ability-to-take-it and its sense-of-outrage into its own design. Open the courtroom door to all who could discover a flaw in the moral armor of a teacher —and contemplate the office of the judge as a mediator between the words of instructors and the consciences of mothers.

If a *causa matris* were to become a weapon against moral wrong, it would be impossible to fix its bounds. In the instant case, Justice McGeehan finds legal harm, not in what Bertrand Russell may say in a City College classroom, but in what he has already said in print. Yet ostracism of the man is not a taboo upon the book. The argument which supports the decree proves too much; to be true to its own logic, the personal ban would be accompanied by a libel against the works. Nor can the norms of law be restricted to the single offense against which they are invoked. All persons whose books upon law, the state, psychology, the economy provoke doubts in an accepted faith should be excluded from the faculty and an action *in rem* should lie against pamphlet and tone of so iniquitous an authorship. If the book reveals the character of the man, surely its pages are not proof against the immoral individual who wrote it. Shakespeare does not curb his licentious characters; Goethe's sex-life did not fall into the elementary formula of Christian marriage; George Eliot was at times slightly confused as to who was her lawful husband. A whole catalogue of learned folk—whose writings have long been the stock in trade of the higher erudition —are subject to such an injunction as that displayed here. It will require a defter stroke than Justice McGeehan can

[8 3]

effect to damn Bertrand Russell and to let the pagan Plato and the Christian Abelard go unscathed; the art of hair-splitting will have to be further refined to sacrifice *Education and the Good Life* and save from the slaughter the Song of Solomon.

It is easy to see why courts, not yet enlightened by Justice McGeehan's opinion, have frowned upon such a form of action as silently he allows.[10] A judicial solicitude for moral scruples can have no finite bounds; it imposes upon legal process the duty of sitting in judgment upon every alleged threat to the character of youth. If, all along the intellectual front, judges are to keep watch and ward, they must speed the return of the Inquisition. At City College there must be nothing said or read about biblical men who looked with lust upon female flesh, about Greek heroes who without leave helped themselves to beauties, about men of the desert who upon Arabian Nights seized moon-faced virgins, about rapes as diverse as those of the Sabine women and of Pope's Lock. But books and villains who make them cannot stand alone; perhaps, as our culture currently goes, they are minor influences in molding the characters of girls and boys. Surely, by the same rationale an action would lie against the newspaper, the magazine, the modern novel, the motion picture. And since as we have it upon the authority of holy writ, verified by Justice Mc-Geehan, that "as a man thinketh in his heart, so he is" and all his works, the doom of the law would have to be visited upon all who as accessories became parties to the filth. A notion of an indignant mother masquerading as a balking taxpayer is a fiction with which the courts cannot afford to

---

[10] The courts have generally been reluctant to interfere with the discretion of Boards of Education. See Comment, "Academic Freedom and the Law" (1937), 46 *Yale Law Journal* 670.

do business. In the instant case the learned judge, completely off his beat, mightily invokes the eternal verities.

A confused awareness that the case is none of his business haunts the bellicose lines of the opinion. Jean Kay has filed her complaint and Justice McGeehan denies a motion to dismiss. Instead of looking into her credentials as a litigant, he proclaims the righteousness of taking the matter away from the Board of Higher Education. But even in so efficacious a court a case cannot go forward on its own steam; nor can the judge on his own motion decree that it must be brought to him. The propriety of party and jurisdiction is elementary; yet it is considered only in the interstices of the opinion. The judge, without reaching for an authority, declares that the appointment of Bertrand Russell is "an insult to the people of the City of New York"; then, using indignation to buck up an absent sequitur, he invites Jean Kay to use the facilities of his court. It is all a judicial version of the old Uncle Remus story. Brer Rabbit escapes from the inescapable by climbing a tree; the act runs against the hero's nature and the *mores* of his tribe; but in the extreme instance there was no other way. The auto-call of self-righteousness prompts the jurist to reverse the Board of Higher Education. *Ergo, itaque,* and therefore, a worthy cause blesses with legal sanction any old plea that is within reach.

If the judge is not overvocal about his right to entertain, he burns with zeal in behalf of the complaint. Society has its way of disbursing discretion among its agencies; policy has it that although mistakes, sometimes serious mistakes, may occur, it is on the whole best to leave matters to bodies appointed by law to handle them. An inkling of this is an aspect of His Honor's omniscience; Justice McGeehan would not allow an appeal to court—even to his own court

[85]

—from every decision of a school board; yet here is an action which obviously cries to heaven for review. He admits that the Board of Higher Education has "sole and exclusive power to select the City College faculty"; he must, accordingly, chalk a line between the Bertrand Russell appointment and others of its kind. In this humane endeavor he essays a number of starts which break down, get lost in their own meanderings, or do the vanishing act; then, rising in his judicial strength, he leads one in triumph to its inevitable *quod erat demonstrandum*. The appointment was in violation of the Constitution of the State of New York—but the Board, composed of upright men and women, thinks otherwise and the question of conformity to the higher law is theirs. The appointee must be a citizen [11]—but the statute allows an exception and it is for the Board to judge circumstances. The distinguished philosopher bears no certificate from a normal school—a defect in subduing the free spirit of inquiry to routine which at Bertrand Russell's age might be indulged, since he is much too old a dog to be taught the up-to-date tricks of teaching. His qualifications were not subjected to competitive examination [12]—some other in a handful of bluebooks might have overtowered the series of volumes in which the story of his competence is written. In all of this the judge demands for the teacher a formal and precise fitness; a kindred demand would level the jurist's art to

---

[11] Justice McGeehan declares that should Bertrand Russell make application for citizenship he would be refused. It may be noted here that the judge believes his own scheme of values to be shared by the naturalization laws.

[12] For further discussion of this aspect of the case, see Comment, "The Bertrand Russell Litigation" (1941), 8 *University of Chicago Law Review* 316; Comment, "The Bertrand Russell Case: The History of a Litigation" (1940), 53 *Harvard Law Review* 1192.

the craft of the case-hound and forbid so creative a contribution as the instant opinion.

As leads encounter barriers, his argument falters and threatens to flicker out. Then a judicial hunch which rises to sheer inspiration suggests the penal code. It is a far cry from Bertrand Russell's unassuming it-seems-to-me to an act of overt crime; yet Justice McGeehan is a crusader, stanch in faith and glands, doughty in verbal adventure. At one end he sets down passages from *What I Believe* and *Education and the Modern World*—abstracted from context and blessed with a judicial gloss—in which Bertrand Russell wonders whether man in all his fumblings has as yet discovered the ultimate answer to the riddle of sex. At the other he places provisions of the criminal code—likewise adorned with his own comment—which outlaw "abduction" and "rape." Then he undertakes to span the yawning gulf with a dialectical bridge. There is set against the appointee no charge of crime, of participation in a conspiracy to commit one, of being an accessory before the fact. Instead an attenuated but highly vocal course of reasoning is strung upon the fragile thread of tendency. The statutes which outlaw rape and abduction seek to protect chaste females under eighteen.[13] As report has it there are at City College no chaste females, over eighteen years of age or under; even worse, there are no females at all.[14] The "personality," then, of the "extraordinary" Bertrand Russell must operate by remote control. It must play entirely

---

[13] A friend in history adds this gloss. A bill was introduced in the legislature of Mississippi back before the Civil War which decreed direful punishment for any who put in jeopardy the virtue of a chaste female. A realistic member from a backwoods county proposed to amend with "chased and cotched."

[14] Women are barred from the School of Liberal Arts, where Dr. Russell would have delivered his lectures, but a few occasionally enter Liberal Arts classes by the back door—through enrollments in other schools.

upon males—whether chaste or unchaste the learned jurist deposeth not, though he does grudgingly admit, as if it had something to do with the case, that some of them have years in excess of eighteen. It is unfortunate that the argument peters out at this point, that the judge does not strip naked the process of corruption by which the teacher's mind corrodes the morals of his pupils. It is, however, not impossible to supply the links essential to the unbroken chain. The student body at City College consists of males, chaste or unchaste, some of them over eighteen, with morals poised so delicately that, if Bertrand Russell expounds mathematics or philosophy,[15] they are impelled to abduct and rape, while if he does not appear in their midst, woman's virtue knows no peril. In the modern world such an Eden of innocence as City College is too precious to allow the serpent to intrude.

A far journey lies between a tentative statement about education and a breach of the penal code; yet the logic of a judge of an inferior court leaps it in an easy stride. Some of us might think that Bertrand Russell's frailty lies in a sheer incapacity to rise to hypocrisy; that with a naïve honesty he recites the inquisitive journeys of his mind while we, more sophisticated folk, erect our screens and say acceptable things. We might plead in extenuation that exposure to a teacher of uncompromising honesty might, in its humble way, have "more to do with forming a student's opinions than many syllogisms." But the learned judge, who thinks well of the law he conscripts to his own point

[15] At the close of the preface of Dr. Russell's latest book, *An Inquiry into Meaning and Truth* (1940), is this comment: "This book would have formed the substance of my lectures at the College of the City of New York, if my appointment there had not been annulled." It is submitted that these recondite lectures on epistemology could hardly result in general demoralization of the student body.

of view, exhibits a more distinctive morality. A thing is to be acclaimed evil if it tends to a fracture of the penal code. It matters not that we live in a culture which has related aspects but no isolated parts. Nor is it of note that every influence plays upon objects which are subject to countless other influences; or that gradually the force of an influence is spent as it takes its way down the maze of human activity. Nor is it relevant that logic has never subdued "tends" into cause; that in philosophy tendency is still at large; that hitherto the law has refused to assess liability or impose punishment by so vague a reference. Yet, for Justice McGeehan, let it be said that he brings the touch of creation to legal judgment. It is not the least among his accomplishments that he rests responsibility upon a ground which logic, philosophy, and the established law have found to be sinking sand.

All this may seem to exhibit an overconcern with the technical issues of party and jurisdiction. But it is in just such procedural matters that the issue of substance lies. It is here that the judge strikes his real blow at academic freedom.[16] In abuse of his judicial trust, he accepts a case he has no right to entertain and makes a decision which does not belong to his court. In behalf of his victim it has been argued that since he is to teach mathematics, the strictures from the bench are beside the point.[17] Such an ar-

---

[16] Note this statement from the opinion of the same Justice McGeehan, *In re Grand Jurors Assn. Bronx County, N. Y., Inc.*, 25 N.Y. Supp. 2d. 154: "Furthermore, the fundamental purpose of the grand jury system is to obtain a group of men and women who represent a fair and impartial cross-section of the citizens of the country; each one with his or her own individual thoughts, experience, and reactions. The preservation of such a complete freedom of thought and expression is essential in order to maintain one of our most sacred institutions."

[17] The legal ordeal was put in further jeopardy by the exercise of discretion within the office of the Corporation Counsel. By law, policy, and sound sense, the last word as to whether a case should be brought

[89]

gument is unfair to Bertrand Russell; its conception of specialty belittles the teacher's calling; it evades the very question of freedom of thought which should be driven home. Justice McGeehan, in usurping an office which does not belong to his court, puts the pursuit of knowledge, upon which all human progress depends, in mortal jeopardy.

If the matter involved Bertrand Russell alone, it would be of concern. If the instance is made general, its significance stands even more sharply out. Let Bertrand Russell be any instructor; let his remarks on sex be any utterance on race, religion, finance, politics, industry, foreign affairs, which is not in lockstep with the symbols which currently circulate as fact; let Jean Kay be any parent-turned-taxpayer for purposes of litigation only, who finds printed passages anathema; let Justice McGeehan be any inferior judge who gets his prejudices and the law all muddled; and over all make the word "tends" pinch-hit for cause in all questions of legal liability—and ask what can be the future of critical inquiry in a democratic land. Like all possessions which enrich human life, morality is a thing to be attained; in respect to it we are as yet little beyond the dark ages. It is too bad that the learned judge has given us very unlearned law. It is far worse that, just as we are painfully fumbling for the tentative, he insists upon serving up a spurious absolute.

---

belongs with the agency which is concerned, not with the official whose task is to act as its legal agent. The attorney may, of course, advise, propose alternative courses of action, and even at the promptings of conscience, retire from the case. But unless the ultimate decision is reserved to the agency primarily concerned, its capacity to discharge its office is impaired and authority tends to be concentrated in an official remote from the field of action. In the instant case the Corporation Counsel was found wanting in energy and resourcefulness. Justice McGeehan was not the only actor out of character in this tragi-comedy.

THE PROBLEMS
OF EDUCATION IN A
DEMOCRACY

By Richard McKeon

The Problems of Education
in a Democracy

I N practical affairs—political, economic, and moral—individual instances have the force of universals, and
problems are generalized in particular occurrences. The
significance of laws is known only in their applications
and in the precedents established by past judgments; and
the use we make of public institutions no less than the
recognition we accord social *mores* is based on calculation,
habitual or conscious, of future contingencies based on convictions best stated in the citation of the occasions when
rights and privileges were endangered, or granted, or lost.
Institutions can be understood only if the history of their
operation and functions is known. They can be preserved
or improved, apart from accident and good fortune, only
if they are understood, while conversely they are most
easily perverted when new pasts and novel applications
are invented for them. Rights and duties, injustices suffered and usurpations imposed may be stated in terms of
principles, but even principles, when they bear on men's
action, thought, and expression, have a date and a local
determination, for they were established in the course of
that adaptation of man's life to the manners, convictions,

[93]

and actions of other men and the life and ends of a community which goes by the name of civilization, and the history of civilization is the history of men and groups in conflict and in co-operation. Experiments in moral philosophy are all *experimenta crucis*, for, unlike the physical sciences in which knowledge and formulae are the final solution to inquiry, knowledge of a social situation supplies only the materials by which to judge what is the case and whether what is should be the case, and frequently, in situations in which the judgment suggests that improvement is desirable, knowledge is complete only after the effort of thought and action has been applied to alter the original situation.

The agitation concerning the person, doctrines, and career of Bertrand Russell which followed his appointment to the staff of the College of the City of New York, the actions of social groups and public officials, the decision in the courts of New York concerning the propriety, wisdom, and legality of the appointment, and the legal and political maneuvers which have followed that verdict, bring to a focus in this case problems that go far beyond issues peculiar to one individual, one college, or one city—and this irrespective of one's judgment concerning the value of Mr. Russell's philosophy, the soundness of his conclusions concerning morality and sex, the sanctity of his life and the salubriousness of his influence on the numerous students who have studied with him. Among these are problems of law and of legal procedure; problems of government and of the rights, functions, and powers of governmental agencies; problems of civil and academic freedom; problems concerning the nature and pursuit of philosophic, scientific, and scholarly inquiry; problems concerning moral, social, and religious truths, the criteria by which

[94]

they are to be recognized, the manner of their propagation, and the effects of their application; problems of the risks and benefits, and even the possibility, of advances in morals and in social relations; problems of power politics, religious propaganda, and the differentiation of traditional values from inbred and obscurantist prejudices. Among the ancient controversies and the uneasy fears which are with ample justification aroused by such a confluence of interests and dangers, however, two problems stand out with peculiar prominence: the problem of moral and religious forces, the efficacy these forces must have and the support they need in a democracy, and the problem of science and teaching, the unusual facilities democracies afford for their encouragement and advancement and the peculiar dependence of democracies on their successful continuance. Moral responsibility and firm commitment to ideals established in the traditions and institutions men have built and preserved, and concern for truth wherever it is found, joined with a readiness to pursue its ramifications and to accept its consequences, are at the same time bases on which democracy is built and accomplishments which are among its chief contributions to the lives of men. Yet they would now seem to be in conflict again, as they have often seemed to be in the past, and it is therefore no grandiose magnification of the issues of the Russell case to compare it with other instances of philosophers and scientists and teachers persecuted in the name of morals and religion, or to see in this instance some of the chief issues of the problem of education in a democracy.

If history is to be consulted on questions involved in the preservation of spiritual values and the increase of knowledge, it is important to discriminate what has been said in praise of religion and science, usually magniloquently and

[95]

magnificently, from what has been done effectively to promote them. The importance of neither is lessened by the recognition that much nonsense has been promulgated in the name and in praise of science and that virtue does not always survive the ministrations of moralists. Yet there is an important difference between the improvement of morality and the pursuit of knowledge. The tests of scientific inquiry, however difficult their application and however frequent the occurrence of errors of judgment and execution, are in the accuracy, verifiability, and significance of its conclusions, and only experts, however much they may at times differ in method and doctrine, are competent to apply or interpret such tests. The problem of spiritual and moral values is more complex, for although examples of moral excellence may, particularly with the lapse of time and the quieting of contemporary controversy, receive almost universal recognition and approbation, there is little agreement among the groups of men, once a few truths about the laws of the land and constitutional rights and duties have been recited, on the criteria by which good is to be discriminated from evil or on the experts competent to apply the criteria and pronounce the judgment. The bearing of the two on problems of education is necessarily different.

An instructor in an institution of higher education should be a competent worker in his field and a competent teacher of his subject; he should preferably be both, or he should have cultivated one to a high degree, sufficient to enable him to make contributions to knowledge in the field of his research or to take a place among the influential and inspiring teachers who turn students to the love of science and culture. The choice of such men is one of the serious responsibilities of the administrations and faculties of schools. All

[96]

men may be said to be involved in the pursuit of values and the cultivation of virtues, not merely in their professional capacities, as teachers or judges or bishops, but as men and as citizens: as individuals they suffer or benefit from the results of their own actions and the effects of the actions of others, and the state in its educational institutions aids them to attain maturity of action and in its legal and penal institutions restrains them from the more obvious and material damages to their own health and sanity and to the rights of others. Moral questions are, however, by their nature easily transformed into oppositions of doctrinal partisanship, whereas scientific questions more rarely, and then usually to the detriment of science, permit long-enduring cliques. In science and philosophy it is possible to separate questions of doctrinal agreement from questions of ability and technical competence, but the suspicion is always justified that hostile criticism of a man's moral and spiritual standards, of his character and influence, conceals unspecified doctrinal differences. Two questions of method and of fact take precedence over properly moral issues in all attempts to impose ethical and spiritual standards if the importance of standards in a community is taken seriously: the general question whether morality and religion can be advanced by enforced acts of conformity and politically engineered acts of suppression and whether custodians of the spirit attain to things of the spirit by posting doctrines and condemning inquiry; and the specific question of the place of intelligence and the intellectual virtues among the moral influences in education, which have a function as custodians of the virtues, recognized by philosophers as different as Aristotle, Spinoza, and Dewey, but seldom considered in those moral crises which are solved by burning books and dismissing scholars.

What has been said and what might be said concerning the appointment of Bertrand Russell to a municipal college furnish concrete illustration of the extremes of variation, in such controversies, of authoritative statement from ascertainable fact. Many philosophers would disagree with Mr. Russell on points of philosophic analysis and doctrine, but few would fail to number him among the greatest of contemporary philosophers. Those who have been associated with him in his teaching are able to testify to his high competence both in the general instruction by which students are introduced to philosophic studies and in the criticism and direction of research which are essential to advanced work. In moral theory, as in mathematical logic, Mr. Russell's speculations have been acute and original. They have been characterized primarily by their frank concern with problems which had arisen in new forms during the postwar generation and which polite moralists preferred to deprecate or ignore; viewed in the context of the sex-practices rather than of the reticences of the times, they are less open to criticism for immorality than for idealism such as characterized the doctrines of Plato or Rousseau among Mr. Russell's intellectual forebears in this difficult field. Such questions, however, are subordinate to the obfuscation of issues involved in the judgment passed on the possible moral and spiritual influence of Mr. Russell. A teacher may influence his students by his character or by his doctrines: Mr. Russell is a man so scrupulous in the examination of his motives and so schooled to consciousness of the consequences of his actions that the student who sought to emulate him should carry over something of those traits as well as some touch of intellectual pertinacity and acumen; Mr. Russell has in recent years been engaged in teaching mathematical logic and related branches of philosophy, and these are subjects in which the illicit loves and the illegitimate relations, so prominent in the statements and apprehensions of his judges and his religious and legal critics, might seem, by considerations of probability or examination of the record of his teaching, to be unlikely subjects and implausible consequences.

Any generalizations suggested by these considerations will reflect the difference of the criteria available in scientific judgments and in value judgments. The standards of truth should be sought by sedulous application to the nature of things: they may be said to be absolute in the sense that what is found to be true is fitted to the body of objective facts distinguished in a commonly experienced universe, and yet the history of the progress of knowledge leaves little warrant for the presumption that any one body of propositions, however long or conscientiously labored, contains the unique expression of truth or that it could be applied, without serious injury to philosophy and science, as the test and criterion of divergent inquiries and studies. The evidence of history apart, it is within the limits of possibility that the grounds of morality are as unambiguous as the natural grounds adduced in evidence for natural laws, and there has been a more confident tendency in morals and religion than in science and philosophy to assert the unique claims of some single body of statements to encompass the truth by which a chosen group of people, lighted by grace or selected by nature or awakened to some moral sensitivity, might accomplish its salvation. Even that possibility, the recognition of which constitutes one of the important precepts of religious tolerance, lends no plausibility to the further supposition that morality or any other social value might be secured by imposing the customs or beliefs of one group as the test to be applied to the intentions or actions of all men, and the history of doctrines is a dreary tale of the deleterious effects of such impositions. Although prophets and saints have found it difficult to justify the ways of God to men or to penetrate the workings of human morality—indeed sometimes because of that difficulty—judgments of things moral and spiritual have frequently pretended to an absoluteness beyond the claims of other branches of human knowledge, and even in science the defense of absolute criteria and the prohibition of false or trivial or useless doctrines have been undertaken more usually for moral than for scientific reasons. These differences suggest a crucial distinction between the criteria relevant to scientific and to moral judgments. In science a doctrine should be abstracted from considerations of times and places and persons to be tested against the subject matter it purports to treat; in moral and religious judgments it is of the utmost importance to consider persons, circumstances, and conditions. When moral and religious reasons are alleged in public condemnations borne against men of science, the truth of the doctrine condemned is seldom directly in question and the reasons for the judgment and its consequences can be found more surely by asking who made the judgment, against whom, for what alleged reasons, and to what actual effects.[1] It is essential, therefore, if one is to

---

[1] On the question of relativity and precision in moral matters the statements of philosophers are numerous: cf. Aristotle, *Nicomachean Ethics*, i. 3. 1094^a12; ii. 6. 1106^a14; *Politics*, iii. 4. 1276^b17. In civil and in canon law like considerations have traditionally been in force to determine the meaning and application of generalizations. Canon lawyers seem historically to have adapted from grammarians and rhetoricians the rule to consider times, places, persons, and conditions in the interpretation of texts; the rule is repeated from Hincmar of Rheims by Bernold of Constance and Ivo of Chartres and passed from legal to philosophic and theological method in the works of Peter Abailard. Cf. Thomas Aquinas, *Summa Theologica*, Ia–IIae, q. 7, a. 2.

recognize in the Russell case the bearings it illustrates of moral and religious judgments on the system of education in a democracy, to consider not merely the importance or the nature of morality in general but also the history of the consequences of similar judgments, which have been unfortunately numerous, in past instances.

II

Among the few surviving bits of consecutive information about the teachers who initiated philosophy and morals in ancient Greece, the tale of persecution, exile, and death on religious, moral, and political charges is a recurrent item. Possibly the same conditions which permit the growth of a free and original philosophy furnish opportunities for bourgeois repressions and popular violence, since Athens, the center of art and culture, was particularly notorious in the record of its intolerances, and in any case thinkers as well as bigots must be prominent in the community if freedom of thought is to be suppressed. Few of the great philosophers associated with Athens escaped suspicion or accusation of impiety and immorality or danger of the death penalty attached to conviction on such charges. With a little malice or ignorance much of philosophy might be construed as denial of God or Providence; moral philosophies in which the adjective "divine" was a simple term of value and the names of the gods almost figures of speech would frequently seem to preach strange religions; almost any statement about local cults involves a criticism of them, and statements about the mystery religions were in antiquity an infraction of law. The contribution of these legal provisions to the welfare of Athens may be judged, in part, by the large number of suspects under them who are remembered for their intellectual and political achievements even more than for the record of their fate at the hands of the state: Anaxagoras suffered condemnation for suggesting that the heavenly bodies were mineral in composition, Protagoras for the agnostic caution of his theology, Socrates for introducing new gods and corrupting the young in a career which has seemed to later generations a model of sanctity, Diagoras of Milos for revealing the Mysteries, Theodorus and Stilpo for atheism, while Aspasia, Aristotle, and Theophrastus barely escaped the consequences of political actions which took the guise of moral and religious judgments. Athens may have been unique in this as in other respects among the Greek states, since the fate of the philosophers seems to have been paralleled in the careers of poets like Euripides and of statesmen like Pericles and Aristides, while in other states doctrines of considerable novelty and skeptical hardiness, far beyond the implications entailed in what Socrates or Protagoras had said, were enunciated by Xenophanes, Parmenides, Heraclitus, and Democritus without apparently stirring popular interest or inspiring official action.

The history of ancient persecutions contributes this guidance among new intolerances, that true piety and wisdom and virtue can be separated from the accidents of doctrines more easily in them, since the truths bitterly defended in the old courts of law no longer arouse such passionate recognition of their importance while the pursuits for which the victim was attacked often continue creditable and their attitudes noble. Old intolerances would seem barbaric and bizarre, if the procedures and motives were not familiar and actual. The injustice and the motivations are poignantly apparent in each of the numerous accounts of Anaxagoras's trial.

[102]

Of the trial of Anaxagoras different accounts are given. Sotion in his *Succession of the Philosophers* says that he was indicted by Cleon on a charge of impiety, because he declared the sun to be a mass of red-hot metal; that his pupil Pericles defended him, and he was fined five talents and banished. Satyrus in his *Lives* says that the prosecutor was Thucydides, the opponent of Pericles, and the charge one of treasonable correspondence with Persia as well as of impiety; and that sentence of death was passed on Anaxagoras by default. When news was brought him that he was condemned and his sons were dead, his comment on the sentence was, "Long ago nature condemned both my judges and myself to death"; and on his sons, "I knew that my children were born to die." . . . Hermippus in his *Lives* says that he was confined in the prison pending his execution; that Pericles came forward and asked the people whether they had any fault to find with him in his own public career; to which they replied that they had not. "Well," he continued, "I am a pupil of Anaxagoras; do not then be carried away by slanders and put him to death. Let me prevail upon you to release him." So he was released; but he could not brook the indignity he had suffered and committed suicide. Hieronymus in the second book of his *Scattered Notes* states that Pericles brought him into court so weak and wasted from illness that he owed his acquittal not so much to the merits of his case as to the sympathy of the judges.[2]

Aspasia was involved in the same political situation, but moral reasons were alleged in her charge as well as impiety.[3] Protagoras was expelled by the Athenians, and a

[2] Diogenes Laertius, *Lives of Eminent Philosophers*, ii. 12–3. In the numerous trials of philosophers recorded by Diogenes, the only acquittal noted is that of Anaxagoras, in at least one version of his trial, and the mocking acquittal of Plato by the Aeginetans (iii. 19).

[3] Plutarch, *Pericles*, 32: "About this time also Aspasia was put on trial for her impiety, Hermippus the comic poet being her prosecutor, who alleged further against her that she received free-born women into a place of assignation for Pericles. And Diopeithes brought in a bill pro-

herald was sent through the city to collect his works from all who had copies in their possession, after which they were burned in the marketplace. This judgment was brought on Protagoras by the opening lines of his treatise *On the Gods,* which he may have read for the first time in Athens at the house of Euripides: "As to the gods, I have no means of knowing either that they exist or that they do not exist. For many are the obstacles that impede knowledge, both the obscurity of the question and the shortness of human life." [4] Aristotle's impiety was found in the honors he paid his friend Hermias in the hymn he composed to commemorate Hermias's death and the inscription he prepared for Hermias's statue. Political motives and scholastic rivalries were doubtless concealed in this accusation, and Aristotle avoided its consequences by fleeing Athens lest, he is said to have remarked, the Athenians sin twice against philosophy. His impious compositions have been preserved and the character of his offense may be judged from the inscription:

---

viding for the public impeachment of such as did not believe in gods, or who taught doctrines regarding the heavens, directing suspicion against Pericles by means of Anaxagoras. The people accepted with delight these slanders. . . . Well, then, Aspasia he begged off, by shedding copious tears at the trial, as Aeschines says, and by entreating the jurors; and he feared for Anaxagoras so much that he sent him away from the city."

[4] *Ibid.,* ix. 51-2, 54. Euripides is also reputed to have been the pupil of Anaxagoras; *ibid.,* ii. 10. *Cf.* Plutarch, *De Placitis Philosophorum,* i. 7. Philostratus attributed Protagoras's theological views to the influence of the Persians; *cf. Lives of the Sophists,* 495: "And when he says that he has no knowledge whether the gods exist or not, I think that Protagoras derived this doctrine from his Persian education. For though the magi invoke the gods in their secret rites, they avoid any public profession of belief in a deity, because they do not wish it to be thought that their own powers are derived from that source. It was for this saying that he was outlawed from the whole earth by the Athenians, as some say after a trial, but others hold that the decree was voted against him without the form of a trial. And so he passed from island to island and from continent to continent, and while trying to avoid the Athenian triremes which were distributed over every sea, he was drowned when sailing in a small boat."

This man in violation of the hallowed law of the immortals
was unrighteously slain by the king of the bow-bearing Persians,
who overcame him, not openly with a spear in murderous combat, but by treachery with the aid of one in whom he trusted.[5]

The attacks on Theodorus and Stilpo were based on remarks
at best shrewd, at worst sophistical, but in either case of a
variety common then as now in the discussions of logicians.[6]
Diagoras's open publication of the Mysteries resulted in a
price put on his head of one talent if he was killed and two
talents if he was taken alive.[7] Theophrastus was so well es-

---

[5] Diogenes Laertius, v. 5–7; Aelianus, *Varia Historia*, iii. 36. According to some of the traditions preserved by Diogenes, Aristotle committed
suicide by drinking aconite to escape persecution. Athenaeus has preserved (xv. 697) one sentence from the *Apology* of Aristotle defending
himself from the imputation read into the hymn that he had wished to
sacrifice to Hermias as to an immortal god.

[6] Diogenes Laertius, ii. 101: "However, Theodorus, sitting on one
occasion beside Euryclides, the hierophant, began, 'Tell me, Euryclides,
who they are who violate the mysteries?' Euryclides replied, 'Those who
disclose them to the uninitiated.' 'Then you violate them,' said Theodorus, 'when you explain them to the uninitiated.' Yet he would hardly
have escaped from being brought before the Areopagus if Demetrius of
Phalerum had not rescued him. And Amphicrates in his book *Upon Illustrious Men* says he was condemned to drink hemlock." *Ibid.*, 116:
"There is a story that he [*sc.* Stilpo] once used the following argument
concerning the Athena of Phidias: 'Is it not Athena the daughter of
Zeus who is a goddess?' And when the other said, 'Yes,' he went on,
'But this at least is not by Zeus but by Phidias,' and, this being granted,
he concluded, 'This then is not a god.' For this he was summoned before
the Areopagus; he did not deny the charge, but contended that the reasoning was correct, for that Athena was no god but a goddess; it was the
male divinities who were gods. However, the story goes that the Areopa-
gites ordered him to quit the city, and thereupon Theodorus, whose
nickname was *Theos*, said in derision, 'Whence did Stilpo learn this? and
how could he tell whether she was a god or a goddess?' But in truth Theodorus was most imprudent, and Stilpo most ingenious."

[7] Cf. *Scholia Aristophantica*, ed. by W. G. Rutherford (London, 1896),
on *Aves*, 1072; vol. I, 518–9. Diagoras, who was in consequence of his
doctrines called the Atheist, fled from Athens: Diodorus Siculus, xii. 6. 7.
Cf. Aelianus, *Varia Historia*, ii. 23. In contrast to the philosophers Aelianus praised the Barbarians (who include Hindus, Celts, and Egyptians)

teemed in Athens that one prosecutor who ventured to cite
him for impiety narrowly escaped punishment himself,[8] yet
even he was forced to leave the country for a time.[9] Sometimes the charge is purely political, as in the case of Zeno of

for never having lapsed into atheism. *Cf.* Maximus of Tyre, *Dissertations*
38; and Cicero, *De Natura Deorum*, iii. 37. 89 ff.

[8] Diogenes Laertius, v. 37.

[9] *Ibid.*, 38: "Although his reputation stood so high, nevertheless for a
short time he had to leave the country with all the other philosophers,
when Sophocles the son of Amphiclides proposed a law that no philosopher
should preside over a school except by permission of the Senate and the
people, under penalty of death. The next year, however, the philosophers
returned, as Philo had prosecuted Sophocles for making an illegal proposal. Whereupon the Athenians repealed the law, fined Sophocles five
talents, and voted the recall of the philosophers, in order that Theophrastus also might return and live as before." *Cf.* Pollux, ix. 42, and
Athenaeus, xii. 610: "Myrtilus said: Then am I not right in hating all
of you philosophers, seeing that you hate literature? You are the persons
whom not only King Lysimachus drove by proclamation from his king-
dom as Carystius declares in his *Historical Notes*, but the Athenians did it
as well. Alexis at any rate, says in *The Horseman:* 'So this is what the
Academy is, this is Xenocrates? May the gods grant many blessings to
Demetrius and the legislators, for they have hurled to 'perdition out of
Attica the men who transmit to our youth the power of discourse as they
call it.' A man named Sophocles also drove out of Attica all philosophers
by decree; against him Philo, a disciple of Aristotle, wrote a speech, after
Demochares, the cousin of Demosthenes, had made a speech defending
Sophocles. And the Romans, too, the most virtuous of men in all things,
cast out the Sophists from Rome on the ground that they corrupted the
young men; later for some reason or other, they took them back. The
comic poet Anaxippus brings out clearly your foolishness when he says
in *Thunder-Struck:* 'Woe's me, you go in for philosophy! But I find philosophers are wise only when it is a matter of words, but when it comes
to actions I see they are fools.' With good reason, therefore, many states,
including especially the Lacedaemonian (so says Chameleon in his work
On Simonides), refuse to permit the teaching either of rhetoric or of philosophy because of the envious strife in which you indulge in your debates,
and because of your untimely arguments; because of which, in fact, Socrates lost his life—he who, in the presence of the very men who were
assigned by lot to jury-duty, used arguments of the most knavish sort,
though his theme was justice; on this account also, Theodorus the atheist
lost his life, and Diagoras was sent into exile; on which occasion, when he
was sailing away, he met with shipwreck; again, Diotimus, who wrote
the books attacking Epicurus, was sought out by Zeno the Epicurean and
put to death, as Demetrius of Magnesia tells us in his *Like-named Poets*."

Elea, who was put to death for plotting the overthrow of a tyrant; [10] sometimes friendship for a philosopher is enough to constitute presumption of guilt; [11] sometimes intolerance took the simple form of denigration of character as in the case of Epicurus.[12]

In the trial and death of Socrates, however, what is accidental to the individual instances of this repeated tale disappears to leave the issues defined with the sharpness one might hope for if Platonic Ideas modeled the conflicts of piety and wisdom as well as the virtues in which conflicts are resolved. The problem is political, both in the lofty sense in which the preservation of law and of virtue is set above any possible grievance of the individual, even at the loss of life itself,[13] and in the more ordinary sense that the trial was doubtless engineered by groups and cliques associated in an interested opposition to Socrates.[14] The charge was impiety and corruption of the youth,[15] and the trial, as

---

[10] Diogenes Laertius, ix. 26–7.

[11] *Ibid.*, v. 79: "At the time when he [*sc.* Demetrius of Phalerum] was being continually attacked in Athens, Menander, the comic poet, as I have also learned, was very nearly brought to trial for no other cause than that he was a friend of Demetrius. However, Telesphorus, the nephew of Demetrius, begged him off."

[12] It is probably in Diotimus's book against Epicurus that the fifty scandalous letters attributed to Epicurus were adduced. *cf.* Diogenes Laertius, x. 3. Diogenes Laertius enumerates the slanderers of Epicurus and his school (*ibid.*, x. 3–8), dismissing them as madmen, numbering the witnesses to his benevolence and piety by whole cities (9–12), and sketching the asceticism of his life. "His piety toward the gods and his affection for his country no words can describe. He carried deference to others to such excess that he did not even enter public life."

[13] *Cf.* Plato, *Crito*, 50A ff.

[14] Diogenes Laertius, ii. 39: "Antisthenes in his *Successions of Philosophers*, and Plato in his *Apology*, say that there were three accusers, Anytus, Lycon and Meletus; that Anytus was roused to anger on behalf of the craftsmen and politicians, Lycon on behalf of the rhetoricians, Meletus of the poets, all three of which classes had felt the lash of Socrates."

[15] *Ibid.*, 40. Socrates himself separates his first and really dangerous accusers, those who attributed scientific curiosity to him, from those who

[107]

reported by Plato, showed that the piety of a god-possessed man came into conflict with the claims and influence of an established tradition primarily because the shrewd and frank inquiry into moral questions inspired by suspicion of unexamined beliefs (which Socrates combined with a personal integrity in the traditional virtues) touched the reticences of education and custom. To direct attention to vicious and imprudent actions, even in the way of criticism of them, is to incur the suspicion of causing them. The morals and the dialectic of Socrates need not be defended here, for the issue does not turn on the truth or the feasibility of a philosophy. The reaction of the Athenians no less than the all but universal judgment of men who have preserved the memory of this trial for more than two thousand years is better indication of its social significance than any estimate of the truth or falsity of what Socrates may have said.[16] The

appeared against him at the trial (*Apology*, 18A ff.); he traces the accusation that he was corrupting the youth to irritation caused by his questioning (23C), the corruption being accomplished by teaching the youth about "the things in the air and the things beneath the earth" (reputedly his scientific interest) and "not to believe in the gods" and "to make the weaker argument the stronger" (23D, 26B).

[16] Diogenes Laertius, ii. 43: "So he was taken from among men; and not long afterwards the Athenians felt such remorse that they shut up the training grounds and gymnasia. They banished the other accusers and put Meletus to death; they honored Socrates with a bronze statue, the work of Lysippus, which they placed in the hall of processions. And no sooner did Anytus visit Heraclea than the people of that town expelled him on that very day. Not only in the case of Socrates but in very many others the Athenians repented in this way. For they fined Homer (so says Heraclides) 50 drachmae for a madman, and said Tyrtaeus was beside himself, and they honored Astydamas before Aeschylus and his brother poets with a bronze statue. Euripides upbraids them thus in his *Palamedes*: 'Ye have slain, have slain, the all-wise, the innocent, the Muses' nightingale.' This is one account; but Philochorus asserts that Euripides died before Socrates." The verdict of posterity for Socrates has been so overwhelming that it is only fair to remark that there has been dissent from it, such as the judgment of Hegel who argued (*Geschichte der Philosophie* [Berlin, 1833], vol. II, 100 ff.) that the application of dialectic to moral

accusers of Socrates were either right in their suspicions of the philosopher or wrong: if they were right, their efforts at suppression were so notoriously unsuccessful as to suggest that suppressive measures are not well suited to combat ideas; if they were wrong, their action and success (fatal to Socrates, whatever the effect on his reputation) mark an extremely important problem for democracies, since it is precisely the outstanding men and the strenuous and original minds who are at once the most likely custodians of the future of the state and the most probable victims of factional jealousies and official follies.

III

In Athens it was the state which acted in accusations of impiety and immorality, and the problems raised by such actions in the Dicastery did not differ in kind from the political problems, faced by Solon or Pericles or Themistocles, arising from the conflict of tradition and novel rational action, or from the signs of national danger which privileged groups saw in any alteration of their status and security, or from the advantage which is always on the side of those who can appeal more readily to tradition in the necessarily rhetorical presentation to the people of the issue between traditionalists and innovators. The judgments bore on good and bad alike, but the record of miscarriages in the enforcement of piety and morality is so long that the account of history could not be righted with forgotten records of condemnations which attained their mark; the reasons alleged were consistently moral and religious; the effect of the con-

---

questions involves a serious danger, since it undermines the sense of sacredness of duty by making it depend on individual conviction, and so introduces subjectivity into morals.

demnations—whether they be interpreted as conditioning or as following from the contemporaneous political situations—was to render impossible or ineffective such informed criticism and rational direction as might have contributed to the welfare of the state. Originally the judgments had to do with particular actions or inferences supposed to be consequent upon philosophic attitudes or positions, but gradually in Hellenistic Greece and in the Roman Republic philosophy and science, and even training in literature and rhetoric, were from time to time proclaimed to be dangerous to religion and morality.[17] In Rome, however, after the early edicts of 161 B.C. and 92 B.C., in which philosophers were associated with rhetoricians in public disapprobation, the Roman reaction to innovations followed a characteristic course. Under the influence of Varro and Cicero, Romans took over and adapted, among other perquisites of trade and conquest, what seemed to them the important aspects of Greek culture, and the doctrinal aspects of intolerance became less conspicuous than the political: politicians advanced in their careers on the ruin of other

---

[17] Suetonius, *On Rhetoricians*, 1: " 'In the consulships of Gaius Fannius Strabo and Marcus Valerius Messala the praetor Marcus Pomponius laid a proposition before the senate. As the result of a discussion about philosophers and rhetoricians, the senate decreed that Marcus Pomponius, the praetor, should take heed and provide, in whatever way seemed in accord with the interests of the State and his oath of office, that they be not allowed to live in Rome.' Some time afterward the censors Gnaeus Domitius Ahenobarbus and Lucius Licinius Crassus issued the following edict about the same class of men: 'It has been reported to us that there be men who have introduced a new kind of training, and that our younger men frequent their schools; that these men have assumed the title of Latin rhetoricians, and that young men spend whole days with them in idleness. Our forefathers determined what they wished their children to learn and what schools they desired them to attend. These innovations in the customs and principles of our forefathers do not please us nor seem proper. Therefore it appears necessary to make our opinion known, both to those who have such schools and to those who are in the habit of attending them, that they are displeasing to us.' " *Cf.* Aulus Gellius, *Noctes Atticae*, xv. 11.

men's reputations and the activities of informers grew into a vast and profitable business in the pursuit of which scientific or philosophic doctrines would be too subtle an instrument for the purposes intended.[18] The adaptation of Greek culture, moreover, seems to have followed in this emphasis on practicality the lines laid in the old opposition of rhetoric and philosophy, for whereas the teaching of rhetoric was endowed by Vespasian and the emperors who followed him, such philosophers as Rome might boast of, among them Epictetus, were expelled from Rome and Italy under Domitian and philosophy was thereafter with difficulty distinguished from sophistic.[19]

The main oppositions of this pragmatic view survived in the development of Christianity in the West, and even before Ambrose borrowed a moral scheme from Cicero and a technique of exegesis from the Greeks, or Augustine laid Platonic foundations for a Christian philosophy, the first adaptations of an older culture to the new religion were attempted by men who were trained rhetoricians. In the practical exigencies involved in the preaching of the new tidings and in the achievement of salvation, philosophic speculation was in part a vanity to be condemned for its uselessness and arrogance, in part a dangerous source of errors to be controverted by Christian arguments. As a result, condemnations of doctrines as immoral and against religion took on a new importance and specificity, for on the one hand the doctrines and the books in which they were expressed, pagan

---

[18] Renan sees in this difference an opposition between inquisitorial practices in Greece and freedom of thought in Rome; cf. *Les Apôtres*, pp. 313 ff.

[19] Suetonius, *Vespasian*, 18. For a statement of the relation of philosophy and rhetoric, cf. Quintilian, i. Pr. 9 ff.; x. 1. 35, 81 ff., 123 ff.; xii. 2. 5 ff. For the interest of the Antonines in rhetoric see Philostratus, *Lives of the Sophists*, 539–40, 557, 559–61, 563, 566–7, 571, etc.

as well as Christian, came to be treated as possessions to be defended by political and legal devices, and on the other hand, though the moral and political dimensions were still referred to, errors were no longer vague departures from tradition but could be stated in single propositions.

Pagan Romans had already reduced the *respublica* to the *res populi* and it was therefore a simple transformation to make the newly predicated things of the spirit property of the Church. The doctrine transmitted by Christ to the apostles and by the apostles to the faithful was theirs to defend from attack and distortion, and dangers in both respects could be found in the methods and doctrines of philosophers; [20] pagans for their part, when the opportunity offered, prohibited the reading of pagan authors by Christians, since they did not credit the authority of the gods who inspired those works and so put the classics to improper

---

[20] For the influence of scriptural authority against pagan philosophers *cf*. R. McKeon, "Aristotelianism in Western Christianity," in *Environmental Factors in Christian History* (Chicago, 1939), 208 ff. Paul is particularly influential in determining the attitude toward faith and "vain philosophy"; *cf*. I Timothy 6:20: "O Timothy, guard that which is committed unto thee, turning away from the profane babblings and oppositions of the knowledge which is falsely so called; which some professing have erred concerning faith." *Cf*. Gal. 1:6; II Peter 2:1. Tertullian early invoked the analogy of Roman law to restrain the Gnostics from use or interpretation of the Scriptures, since they were by *longae possessionis praescriptio* the possession of the Churches; *Liber de Praescriptionibus adversus Haereticos*, 20–1; PL 2, 31–2. The opposition is clear to his mind between the poor truths of philosophers and divine truth: *cf. ibid.*, 7; PL II, 20–1: "*Fuerat Athenis, et istam sapientiam humanam, affectatricem et interpolatricem veritatis, de congressibus noverat, ipsam quoque in suas haereses multipartitam varietate sectarum invicem repugnantium. Quid ergo Athenis et Herosolymis? Quid Academiae et Ecclesiae? Quid haereticis et Christianis? Nostra institutio de Porticu Salomonis est, qui et ipse tradiderat* Dominum in simplicitate cordis esse quaerendum. *Viderint, qui stoicum et platonicum et dialecticum Christianismum protulerunt. Nobis curiositate opus non est, post Christum Jesum; nec inquisitione, post Evangelium.*" For the relation of property to spiritual goods in Augustine, *cf*. R. McKeon, "The Development of the Concept of Property in Political Philosophy," *Ethics*, XLVIII (1938), 316 ff.

uses; [21] and when finally the Church became in effect the preserver and custodian of pagan culture in the West, the justification was that the arts were instruments assigned as proper labor for the pagans by divine grace and foresight but for Christian uses and therefore were taken over as property by their rightful owners.[22] Both tendencies were based on past movements and were to continue in the future. The simple legal opposition of the doctrines of the Christians and the disciplines of the pagans, on the one hand, continued the battle of rhetoric with philosophy, which, together with the confusing of rhetoric and sophistic and the merging of both with the religious philosophy of Neoplatonism, were the outstanding philosophic phenomena of the later Empire. The statement of precise doctrines, on the other hand, and the marshaling of arguments in their defense, particularly against the background of an increasing erudition in philosophy, raised to prominence questions of method and principle which would require for their solution all the resources of dialectic and philosophy. Together they are the two positions which have continued in the history of heresies and dogmas to the present day, the one requiring a blanket condemnation of reason, or philosophy, or science as doomed to error or insufficiency or uselessness in contrast to a loftier and superrational truth, and therefore in need, for adaptation to new circumstances, of little more than institutional and procedural changes; the other the searching out and anathematizing of specific doctrines in-

---

[21] Julian, *Epistle 36*.

[22] The common form of argument, much repeated during the Middle Ages, was that Christians were justified in making use of the works of the pagans much as the chosen people had appropriated the possessions of the Egyptians, particularly since the appropriation from the philosophers of statements suited to the Christian faith was as from unjust possessors; cf. Augustine, *De Doctrina Christiana*, ii. 40, 60–1 PL XXXIV, 63.

consistent with or dangerous to that truth, and therefore involved in an accelerating development in range of doctrines and subtlety of discrimination. The two are originally in opposition concerning the propriety and manner in which human reason might be used in the interpretation of divine truths, but as the scope of errors inconsistent with theological truths is extended they emerge finally in co-operation.

Both hypotheses are within the limits of possibility: human reason may be committed to error except as lighted by a supernatural illumination, and certain ends of man and certain truths essential to those ends may exceed the evidence available to reason in this life or experience on this earth. Granted the possibility that such truths have been delivered to man or to certain men, it would of course be of the utmost importance to those who held them to preserve the purity and precision of their statement, to gain as much respect for them as possible, and to promulgate them in the fashion they seem to deserve. The truths themselves and the agencies empowered to interpret them may be clearly established in the formulae which emerge in the formation of such a tradition: answers to questions concerning what the doctrines are and who determines their significance seem innocent, until their implications in the history of civilization are traced to the measures used to spread truths which are more important than life itself, and through the multitude of motives and interests which have been concealed behind inscrutable symbols. The history of heresies is a massive expansion in doctrines and victims of the sporadic persecutions of antiquity, and naturally enough censures are most widespread and haphazard in their incidence precisely when the pursuit of art, science, and philosophy becomes vigorous. The shift from antiquity to the Middle Ages is epitomized in the significances which the word *heresy* has received: originally it meant simply a *taking* as of a city or a material object;[23] later it meant the political, literary, philosophic, or religious sect to which one adhered;[24] finally it meant the choice of a doctrine and the setting of one's own opinion against the received dogma and the authority and unity of the Church.[25] Even if this opposition of a commonly held truth endangered by individual deviations from it is accepted, the long history of attempts to promulgate such truths suggests, quite apart from the question whether they are in fact truths, two considerations: first the question of the success of these attempts in discriminating error from truth, and this is best treated—at least until the effects of illumination are universal—by considering the persons attainted in condemnations, the continued influence of the condemned error, and the effect of the procedure on inquiry; second the question of the actual agency which determines the error, the reasons for the determination, and the influences which might affect it.

The history of heresies might be written largely in terms of the regrets stimulated by the men and doctrines condemned, for even if it is granted that the hypothesis of a unique truth is at least tenable, the evidence of history lends more plausible support to the hypothesis that within the range of human ability and the effort of human sincerity

---

[23] Herodotus, iv. 1; ix, 3; Thucydides, ii. 75. 1; Aristotle, *Politics*, i. 8. 1256ᵃ26, etc.

[24] Sextus Empiricus, *The Outlines of Pyrrhonism*, i. 16; Diogenes Laertius, i. 19; Josephus, *Antiquitates Judaicae*, xiii. 5. 9; *De Bello Judaico*, ii. 8. 1, 2.

[25] Irenaeus, *Contra Haereses*, i. I. 1; iii. 11. 9; 12. 11–2; PG VII, 438, 890, 905, 906; Tertullian, *De Praescriptionibus*, 6 and 27; PL II, 18, 50–1; Cyprian, *De Unitate Ecclesiae*, PL IV, 500; Jerome, *In Epistolam ad Galatas*, PL XXVI, 417; *In Epistolam ad Titum*, PL XXVI, 598; Augustine, *De Baptismo contra Donatistas*, v. 26; PL XLIII, 186–7. Isidore of Seville, *Etymologiae*, vii. 3; PL LXXXII, 296.

doctrines must take many forms, and the testimony of later experts in logic, philosophy, religion, science, and theology favoring condemned propositions must have its due weight. Apart from counter-hypotheses concerning truth, however, there remains the question of effectiveness: the numerous heresies into which the early defenders of the new religion fell by a curious fatality and the even more expertly articulated theologies which served as counterpoise to the ancient doctors of the Church in their expositions of the true doctrine, did not cease with the measures that suppressed their proponents; rather the need for recurring to the old names is frequent in later centuries, and refurbished prototypes of rejected doctrines are in many instances still held today. Moreover, the machinery of censure and condemnation makes discussion less effective in defense of doctrines than the tricks of politics and sophistry. Accidents of circumstance or the power of protectors, ecclesiastical or lay, may save the innovator from the consequences of his pious intentions, as they did in the case of John Scotus Eriugena or Berengar of Tours; pious followers may with no great difficulty rectify the errors of an original master and still be powerless to save the repute of his doctrine or openly extend the influence of his method, as seems to have been the case with four disciples of Peter Abailard; and other men might escape, by political ingenuity or weight of learning, the consequences of comparable doctrines in almost identical situations, as Abailard's master Thierry of Chartres succeeded in turning off the zeal of their common critic, St. Bernard.

Not only does anathematized error continue unchecked by such procedures, not only is the competent pursuit of the tasks of philosophy and science threatened and impeded, but the same dangers are extended to the correct interpretation of the true doctrine, and the most sanctified expression

may, with the lapse of time and the variation of usage, develop unsuspected ambiguities. Saints can be saved from
suspicion of manifest but newly discovered heresies only
by ingenious word-tinkering, the benefits of which, however, are seldom extended to heretics. Thomas Aquinas has
made a shrewd statement of this process of doctrinal trans-
lation.

That some things are found in the statements of the ancient
Greek Fathers which seem to be doubtful to moderns, I think
arises from two causes. First, because the errors which had arisen
about faith gave the holy doctors of the Church occasion to
present those things which belong to faith with greater circum-
spection, in order to eliminate those errors. Thus it is obvious
that the holy doctors who lived before the Arian error did not
speak so exactly concerning the unity of the divine Essence as
the doctors who came after, and the same thing happens in other
errors, as is apparent not only in the various doctors, but particularly in the greatest of the doctors, Augustine. For in the works
that Augustine wrote after the heresy of the Pelagians had arisen,
he spoke more cautiously of the power of free will than in the
books which he wrote before the rise of the aforesaid heresy.
In those books, defending the freedom of the will against the
Manichaeans, he made some statements which the Pelagians,
opposing divine grace, quoted in defense of their error. And so
it is not surprising if modern doctors of faith, writing after the
rise of various errors, speak more cautiously and, as it were, more
elaborately concerning the doctrine of faith in order to avoid all
heresy. Whence if some things are found in the statements of the
ancient doctors which are not said with as much caution as is
used by moderns, they should not be despised or rejected, but
neither should we continue them, but rather interpret them rev-
erently. Second, because many statements which have a correct
significance in the Greek language may not have a correct
significance in Latin, since Latins and Greeks confess the same

[117]

truth of faith in different words. Thus the Greeks say rightly and catholicly that the Father and the Son and the Holy Spirit are three hypostases, but among the Latins it would be incorrect to say that they are three substances, although *hypostasis* is the same among the Greeks as *substance* among the Latins. But *substance* is more commonly used in the sense of *essence*, which the Greeks like us confess to be one in God. For this reason, while the Greeks speak of three hypostases, we speak of three persons. Nor is there any doubt that it is the same in many other cases.[26]

Moreover, the doctrines of Aquinas themselves, notwithstanding their later reputation for truth and sanctity, were subject to long and bitter attacks, and several of them were in danger of condemnation during his lifetime, while a larger number of them were condemned after his death at the universities of Paris and Oxford.[27] The manner in which

---

[26] *Contra Errores Graecorum. Prologus.* The same dialectical emendation may be applied to ancient philosophy; cf. *Summa Theologica*, Ia, q. 84, a. 5: "As Augustine says, 'If those who are called philosophers have by chance said anything true and accommodated to our faith, we must appropriate it from them as from unjust possessors for our use. For some of the doctrines of the gentiles contain simulated and superstitious fictions which each of us must avoid when we go out from the society of gentiles.' Consequently whenever Augustine, who was imbued with the doctrines of the Platonists, found anything in their statements accommodated to the faith, he took it over; but those things which he found contrary to our faith he changed into a better form." Cf. *ibid.*, IIa–IIae, q. 23, a. 2, ad 1.

[27] Only Thomas's return to Paris saved two of his propositions from the list condemned at the University of Paris in 1270: cf. P. Mandonnet, *Siger de Brabant et l'Averroïsme Latin au XIIIᵐᵉ siècle*, 2ème éd. (Paris, 1911), vol. I, pp. 106 ff.; M. M. Gorce, *L'Essor de la Pensée au Moyen Age: Albert Le Grand—Thomas d'Aquin* (Paris, 1933), pp. 152 ff. A large number of his doctrines are enumerated—as are even more of the doctrines of Roger Bacon—among the 219 propositions condemned in Paris on March 7, 1277; cf. *Chartularium Universitatis Parisiensis*, ed. H. Denifle and A. Chatelain (Paris, 1899), vol. I, pp. 543 ff.; Mandonnet, *op. cit.*, pp. 214 ff.; Gorce, *op. cit.*, 167 ff. For attempted identifications of the authors of the doctrines condemned in 1277, cf. C. DuPlessis d'Argentré, *Collectio Judiciorum de Novis Erroribus* (Paris, 1728), vol. I, Part I, pp. 204 ff. The scope of subject matter covered in these

the theses of Aquinas were involved in later condemnations is explained in some detail in an interesting document drawn up by Cardinal Peter d'Ailly, himself a philosopher of the first importance and himself suspect of error, to explain the condemnation pronounced against fourteen propositions ascribed to John of Monzon. John had alleged among other points in his defense that his conclusions were derived from the doctrines of St. Thomas which the Faculty of Theology at Paris had expressly commended, which Bishop Stephen had approved, and which Pope Urban V had promulgated as the veridical and Catholic doctrine. Peter argues that the doctrine of St. Thomas had never been so approved as to impede condemnation, but although he and his colleagues had declared thousands of times, to no avail apparently, that they did not reprove the doctrine of St. Thomas in their condemnation, he appends a convenient list of four examples of the errors of St. Thomas.[28] It would be most arrogant to insist that one believe the doctrine of Aquinas to be free of errors.[29] Peter's learned commentary and argument, necessitated by the review of the faculty's judgment by Clement VII, makes somewhat clearer the legal considerations that lay behind the numerous condemnations, usually published as a simple list of erroneous propositions, since the doctrines criticized are for the most part suppressed so completely that the original meaning of the propositions is not always easy to reconstruct, but the explanations serve only to reinforce the doubt, suggested by the vast literature

condemnations may be judged by the fact that when a similar list of erroneous propositions was published with similar intentions in Oxford on March 18, eleven days after the Paris condemnations, the propositions are divided according to subject matter: four in grammatical questions, ten in logic, and sixteen in natural philosophy; cf. *Chartularium*, vol. I, pp. 558–60.

[28] *Collectio Judiciorum*, vol. I, Part II, pp. 75, 82–4.

[29] *Ibid.*, p. 118.

of those condemnations, that the judicial pronouncements of faculties and bishops are not the most precise or effective way to detect or correct errors. John of Monzon was excommunicated on January 27, 1389; he gave proof of his orthodox zeal by writing a violent treatise in defense of the methods employed in electing the popes of Avignon.

The list of philosophers condemned for heresy or error or threatened by such condemnation during the fourteenth, fifteenth, and sixteenth centuries is long and distinguished, and the reconstruction of the doctrines briefly indicated in their proscription and the consideration of the later fortunes of like doctrines is fascinating philosophic and historical speculation.[30] Since philosophic truth is not in question here, but only the devices by which it may be reconciled to an-

---

[30] *Cf.* the collection of "various errors of philosophers" made by the Faculty of the University of Paris in 1290 (*Collectio Judiciorum*, vol. I, Part I, p. 238); or A. Pelzer, "Les 51 articles de Guillaume Occam censurés en Avignon en 1326," in *Revue d'Histoire Ecclésiastique*, XVIII (1922), pp. 240–70; or the pronouncements of the University of Paris against the logical doctrines of William of Ockham and his followers in 1339, reiterated in the Royal edict of 1473 against nominalists with specification of some of the followers: Gregory of Rimini, John Buridan, Peter d'Ailly, Marsilius of Inghen, Adam Dorp, Albert of Saxony (*Collectio Judiciorum*, vol. I, Part I, pp. 337 ff.); or the letter of Clement VI in 1346 on the doctrines of recent philosophers and theologians (*Chartularium*, vol. II, pp. 587 ff.); or the fifty propositions—dealing largely with the ethical consequences of divine causality and theological determinisms—of John of Mirecourt condemned by the Faculty of the University of Paris in 1347 (*ibid.*, pp. 610 ff.); or the errors of Raymond Lully collected in 1290 (*Collectio Judiciorum*, vol. I, Part I, pp. 246 ff.); or the reiteration by the Faculty in 1348 of the papal condemnation of the propositions of Nicholas of Autrecourt, who has been compared with Hume for his criticism of the doctrines of causality and substance and with Bradley for his criticism of the logic of relations (*Collectio Judiciorum*, vol. I, Part I, pp. 355 ff.), and of whose condemnation Peter d'Ailly wrote that "many doctrines were condemned against him because of envy which were none the less later publicly confessed in the schools." These suggestions, of course, constitute only a partial list of the activities of the late thirteenth and early fourteenth century; if extended they would involve the major portion of the philosophers of the period, and much the same task might be undertaken for later periods.

other truth, the extension of those devices both in the agencies which might exercise them and the doctrines to which they apply is striking. Not only popes, but bishops and even the doctors on the faculties of universities exercise the power, and Peter d'Ailly's communication to Clement VII contains a defense of that extension of power worked out in three meticulously developed syllogisms.[31] The categories of doctrinal censure are in like fashion extended into many sub-species, and Melchior Cano (to instance one of the older and therefore simpler classifications) is at pains to differentiate heresy from propositions which are erroneous, offensive to pious ears, temerarious, or scandalous.[32] It is relevant to the thesis which all this history is adduced to support that the extension of the scope of condemnations has been restricted in respect to the agencies empowered to censure doctrines. On March 2, 1679, Innocent XI prohibited theologians from pronouncing on propositions or doctrines prior to the publication of the decision of the Holy See.[33] So far as doctrine is concerned, however, any inquiry or subject matter or discipline may still fall under condemnation.

IV

In the Middle Ages piety and morality were judged by the ecclesiastical power in its various forms and manifestations rather than by the state and the parties and factions that control its course; the condemnations, so far as they

---

[31] *Collectio Judiciorum*, vol. I, Part II, pp. 76–7.
[32] *De Locis Theologicis*, Book XXII, Ch. 11 (Louvain, 1564), pp. 764 ff.
[33] H. Denzinger, *Enchiridion Symbolorum Definitionum et Declarationum de Rebus Fidei et Morum*, n. 1216, 11th ed. (St. Louis, 1911), p. 355. This prohibition is appended to a list of sixty-five errors in moral matters.

bore on teachers, scientists, and philosophers, were usually stated in particulars and enumerated in propositions rather than alleged broadly by reference to strange gods introduced or unfortunate effects worked on the young. In two respects, however, pagan and Christian practices are strictly comparable: condemnation or threat of condemnation by papal court or university faculty fell, like the inquisitional procedures of the Dicastery, on some of the ablest philosophers of the time, and both procedures were ineffective in the extirpation of error. Efforts to preserve the moral integrity and spiritual purity of a people oscillate between two extremes, at which they appear, first as political actions directed to the good of the state and its citizens, and again as doctrinal corrections directed to the preservation of the purity of faith and the salvation of souls. The ends are important; it may be doubted whether the means are adapted to achieve either politically or spiritually desirable ends; there is no doubt that the means frequently conceal motives and lead to actions more noxious to religion and morality than any of the results of intellectual inquiry and criticism. The enumeration of erroneous propositions might seem to insure caution, precision, and to that extent justice in the adjudication of problems of truth and propriety; but since the determination of the error is on principles which cannot be questioned and by inferences which are not stated, the condemnations appeal less to the understanding than to fears and the passions.[34] Even apart from perversions due

---

[34] The errors are not controverted; they are merely enumerated, frequently in terms which are not easy to relate to the original; the condemnation takes the form of an anathema usually expressed with a vigor which is doubtless justified by the heinousness of the errors but hardly calculated to affect the intellect. Thus, to take a more recent example, when Quesnel was condemned by Clement XI for Jansenism in 1713, 101 errors were enumerated, usually in a single sentence each, and then "declared and damned as false, captious, evil-sounding, offensive to pious

to the substitution of other motives for the avowed ends and apart from miscarriages in the effects, such devices for advancing sanctity and morality are totally inconsistent with democracy, even in the extreme case of convictions on the part of a majority that there are absolute truths and selection by that majority of one or more persons to determine or interpret them. The haphazard and individual persecutions of ancient Athens are the natural dangers and disturbances of a democracy: they must be met within the framework of democratic procedures if the democracy is to continue, and to that end freedom, in which even truth may be discovered, rather than truth which slips easily into error in human expressions of it, must be inculcated by education, demonstration, and persuasion. But general pronouncements handed down as necessary consequences of a unique truth necessarily imposed, although they have the human chance of being true, cannot rely on the devices of human proof, and so, transcendentally true or patently false, are potential menaces to the individual and intermittent threats to the state.[35]

---

ears, scandalous, pernicious, temerarious, injurious to the Church and its practice, and not only in respect of the Church but in respect of the secular power contumelious, seditious, impious, blasphemous, suspect of heresy and savoring that heresy and even promoting heresies and heretics and schism, erroneous, proximate to heresy, many times condemned, and finally heretical, manifestly innovating in the line of various heresies and especially those which are contained in the famous propositions of Jansen and indeed taken in the very sense in which these were condemned" (Denzinger, *Enchiridion*, n. 1451, p. 379). Augustine pointed out that it was altogether impossible or at any rate very difficult to define heresy; he called attention to the vast diversities in the lists of heresies, and therefore laid emphasis, as has continued to be the case in canon law, on the obstinate temper with which the wrong opinion is defended. For all the apparatus of propositions and authorities the basic human qualities which enter such condemnations are the same as operated with little apparatus earlier and later than the institution of councils, ecclesiastical courts, and inquisitions.

[35] Freedom of conscience would permit particular groups to subject

Since the Reformation, truth and piety have been sought in religion not by imposition of what is conceived to be best, but by a slowly increasing spread of freedom to follow the dictates of one's own conscience within the limitations only of the rights and duties of citizens. Like the pursuit of happiness which Aristotle found all men agreed was the end of life, obedience to the will of God must seem to all men essential to the good life, but there have been vast differences among men concerning what happiness consists in and what the will of God decrees, and freedom of decision is the one alternative to a unanimity which does not achieve happiness within the possibilities of human determinations and would put the will of God to shame before human judgments.[36]

---

themselves voluntarily to the imposition of such a unique truth, and groups so constituted would be in the position, which should be of interest to modern logicians in their concern with the vicious circle fallacy, of using that freedom to deny that any alternate to their choice is freedom. Cf. the *Syllabus or Collection of Modern Errors* of Pius IX (1864), in which one of the errors noted is the supposition that every man is free to embrace and profess any religion he may think, guided by the light of reason, to be true (Denzinger, *Enchiridion*, n. 1715, p. 467); or the prohibition of Leo XIII (1888) to seek, defend, or enlarge in any way "the promiscuous liberty of religions" (*ibid.*, n. 1932, p. 514); or his reiteration (1899) of this principle to Cardinal Gibbon with specific application to "Americanism" (*ibid.*, n. 1967–76, pp. 528–31); or the pronouncements of Pius X (1907) on erroneous modern doctrines of philosophers and historians (*ibid.*, n. 2071–2109, pp. 545–80).

[36] The painful circularity, cut only by assumptions of infallibility or authoritative statements of conclusions, of all such reasoning has been pointed out repeatedly by philosophers. Cf. J. Bentham, *An Introduction to the Principles of Morals and Legislation*, Ch. II, par. 18 (Oxford, 1907), pp. 21–2: "The *will* of God here meant cannot be his revealed will, as contained in the sacred writings: for that is a system which nobody ever thinks of recurring to at this time of day, for the details of political administration: and even before it can be applied to the details of private conduct, it is universally allowed, by the most eminent divines of all persuasions, to stand in need of pretty ample interpretations; else to what use are the works of those divines? . . . It is plain, therefore, that, setting revelation out of the question, no light can ever be thrown upon the standard of right and wrong, by any thing that can be said upon the question, what is God's will. We may be perfectly sure, indeed, that what-

Religions have been permitted peacefully to break into sects and denominations, yet the epithets "infidel," "atheist," "materialist," and "agnostic" have been used with no more discrimination notwithstanding their less universal or immediate effect. The incidence of such epithets has continued haphazard and unfortunate. Spinoza, who has aptly been called a God-intoxicated man, is one of the great "atheists" of the seventeenth century, and fear of the restrictions which an academic position might put on his philosophic activities led him to decline a professorship at the University of Heidelberg.[37] Bruno, Cardanus, Campanella, Descartes, Hobbes, Locke, Fénelon, Gassendi, Pascal, Newton, so the list runs in the seventeenth century, and its continuation through the eighteenth and nineteenth centuries would omit few important names in philosophy or science.

Though they have followed divergent tendencies in modern times, the political and factional anathematizing which has accompanied freedom and democracy and the doctrinal prescriptions which are possible only with a unique truth and a unique authority have in the past been united, notwithstanding their apparent oppositions, and are being united again today. Unique political and social truths are

---

ever is right is conformable to the will of God: but so far is that from answering the purpose of showing us what is right, that it is necessary to know first whether a thing is right, in order to know from thence whether it be conformable to the will of God."

[37] Epistolae XLVII and XLVIII (*Opera Omnia*, ed. C. Gebhardt [Heidelberg, 1924], vol. IV, pp. 234-6). Spinoza says, in detailing his reasons for declining the post: "I think, in the second place, that I do not know within what limits that freedom of philosophizing ought to be confined in order that I may not appear to disturb the publicly established religion. For schisms arise not so much from an ardent zeal for religion as from men's various passions or the love of contradiction, through which they are wont to distort and to condemn all things, even those that have been correctly stated. I have already experienced these things while leading a private and solitary life; how much more should I have to fear them after I shall have risen to this degree of dignity."

being promulgated which entail doctrinal commitments as definite as any religious dogmatism. The combination of such truths with aspirant absolutisms of moral practice, social and economic establishment, or religious doctrine and observance in unstable and mutually unsafe partnership is the great threat to democracy and the great problem of higher education in democracies. The problems of secondary education are not separate from the social problems of the community, and in general, with due allowance for temporal lags, the school system reflects the character of the community. Higher education, on the contrary, should be controlled by other considerations than what is commonly accepted and should provide training for leaders in the community equipped with sufficient flexibility of judgment to perceive problems and provide for their solution rather than depend on that dilatory attachment to what has always been which leaves resolution of problems to forces which will, in the process, wreck the community. For all the vaunted freedom of thought and expression, independence of thought has never been stimulated or encouraged in America.[38] When the tendency to conformity is so ingrained, it is safe to make strenuous efforts to examine the tradition and to call it into question wherever it seems questionable:

---

[38] *Cf.* J. S. Mill, "M. de Tocqueville on Democracy in America," *Dissertations and Discussions: Political, Philosophical, and Historical,* (Boston, 1864), vol. II, p. 118: "It is the complaint of M. de Tocqueville as well as of other travelers in America, that in no country does there exist less independence of thought. In religion, indeed, the varieties of opinion which fortunately prevailed among those by whom the colonies were settled have produced a toleration in law and in fact extending to the limits of Christianity. If by ill fortune there happened to be a religion of the majority, the case would probably have been different. On every other subject, when the opinion of the majority is made up, hardly any one, it is affirmed, dares to be of any other opinion, or at least to profess it." *Cf.* Matthew Arnold, *Culture and Anarchy*, Preface (New York, 1905), p. xxii.

even if the conclusion of the inquiry reaffirms the tradition, the end is achieved, for education in a democracy cannot be directed to a truth recited by rote and imposed by indoctrination, or force, or even bare custom. To acquiesce in an unexamined or inscrutable tradition is only a stage or two from acquiescence in a despotically imposed political system with its characteristic remedy for the inefficiencies and uncertainties of democracy. In such a system science has the unique task of demonstrating truths known apart from science and discovering devices useful to the prosecution of the ends of the state; education has the task of inculcating those truths and training to those ends. The issue is clear in these terms. To the efficiency with which despotism may seem to enforce accepted truths and work toward accepted ends, democracy opposes, not efficiency in arriving at some other single answer, but such considerations of justice as suggest that the ends of men are better achieved by permitting them a maximum of freedom in the election of those ends, even with the danger that they may be mistaken, and such considerations of truth as suggest that knowledge is better advanced by free inquiry than by constant efforts for the statement of a unanimity. Democracy depends on the freedom of opinion and action which permits experts to investigate problems unhampered by preconceptions and on the broad utilization of the knowledge which results from such investigations to the furtherance of individual opportunity and the common good. Education in a democracy should be engaged in teaching the truths and probabilities so established, together with the grounds that have been advanced in their support and the objections that have been adduced against them; such teaching furnishes a foundation for the responsible exercise of the freedom of speech and opinion which is indispensable to the democratic processes and a basis for the training of

[127]

scholars and scientists in which democracy finds at once an important function and its chief defense.

Three kinds of questions are possible, and history furnishes many actual examples of them, in choosing men to participate in higher education so conceived: questions bearing on their ability, questions bearing on their doctrines and beliefs, and questions bearing on their conduct. Of these the questions of the first group, designed to select men of promise or achievement in research and teaching, are of crucial importance to the system of education and to the state in which it functions; doubtless sufficient care is not exercised and devices for selection are imperfect, but they can be improved only by men trained in the processes of teaching and in the subject matters taught, and failing vigilance on those points no substitute devices or alternative criteria will be effective. The history of higher education in America has worked slowly in three hundred years from the scrutiny of a man's doctrines, personal or professional, to determine his competence as a teacher; [39] the process is far from complete, for it would be arrantly false to suppose that a man's religion may not stand even today in the way of his employment in a college or university, but at least a teacher is rarely dismissed—and then not without active signs of widespread disapprobation—because of his subscription to the articles of a confession or his acceptance of evolution. The danger has moved from questions of what a man believes to ques-

---

[39] A. D. White remarks in the course of discussing problems encountered in founding Cornell University (*A History of the Warfare of Science with Theology in Christendom*, 3rd ed. [New York, 1930], vol. I, p. vii): "It required no great acuteness to see that a system of control which, in selecting a Professor of Mathematics or Language or Rhetoric or Physics or Chemistry, asked first and above all to what sect or even to what wing or what branch of a sect he belonged, could hardly do much to advance the moral, religious, or intellectual development of mankind."

[128]

tions of what he has said or done; the greater proportion of dismissals in institutions of higher education can be traced to some alleged irregularity in the private morality or some heterodoxy in the public actions of teachers. The actions criticized need not have taken place and the influence anticipated may have been without example, for inference is easy from what a man has said about established customs and institutions to conclusions concerning how he would act or how his students must develop, and the willingness to consider heterodoxies, to read books conventionally proscribed, and to examine problems the rumor of whose existence is a threat to the established order may be taken as complicity with the forces which produced those movements, books, and problems. The oppressions which attended the censure of doctrines and beliefs may be made to operate surreptitiously in criticism of a man's morality and his social doctrines with all the specificity of doctrinal selection that characterized medieval condemnations and all the disastrous appeal to popular passions that characterized the unfortunate repressions of antiquity.

These are important truths—moral, social, and religious —and more than any other states democracies must seek and cultivate them. They are, however, truths which are found and shared only as the minds of men are led to them, and they are not defended by decree, or proclamation, or pressure. The virtues essential to the democratic form of government are not sheltered or mysterious growths, and they must be developed, if at all, in the conditions which test them. In morals and in politics, as in religion, values can be cultivated in a democracy by stimulating men to a concern with them, not by announcing and enforcing them. If values cannot be achieved with freedom of thought and opinion, then the whole system of values associated with science and democracy will be destroyed in whatever morality is preserved. Apart from the restrictions put on all men and all citizens, no further moral prescriptions are needed in the selection of instructors for higher education in a democracy; even more, their use endangers the true principles of morality when immorality is really in question, and they are in all cases a ready instrument of interference in inquiry and science. If any lesson is taught unambiguously by the long history of morality by suppression, it is that freedom of thought and of expression are not only privileges consistent with the integrity of a people and a state, but that they are indispensable means for the defense of free institutions and the advancement of a responsible and enlightened morality.

A SCANDALOUS DENIAL
OF JUSTICE

By Morris R. Cohen

A Scandalous Denial
of Justice

Nullius liber homo capiatur . . . aut aliquo modo distruatur . . . nisi per legale judicium parium. . . .
—MAGNA CHARTA, sec. 39

THE legal systems of all modern civilized people recognize the fallibility of judges of first instance, and therefore make provision for appeal and review. And our judicial statistics show that in a high proportion of cases the rulings of the first court have in fact been declared erroneous. The denial of the right of appeal is, therefore, a denial of justice. Such a denial is all the more grievous if it is due to pressure from a political source interfering with the due course of judicial proceedings.

In a number of famous instances, such as the Dreyfus case, enlightened public conscience was properly outraged by the fact that the accused did not receive a fair trial. For on the fairness of judicial procedure depends that security against baseless charges which is indispensable for dignified civilized life. But in the case of Bertrand Russell an internationally honored teacher, scholar, and philosopher was foully condemned, branded as a criminal, and ignominiously deprived of his position as a professor by a proceeding which had not the barest resemblance to a trial.

[133]

The reader will find in the *Harvard Law Review* of May 1940 a brief but incisive legal critique of the irregularity of Judge McGeehan's procedure and the absurdity of the unprecedented doctrines on which his decision rested. But it does not require much legal learning to see that the most elementary requisite of just judicial procedure is violated when a man is condemned without being given a chance to be heard, to confront his accusers, and to offer evidence in refutation of their disingenuous charges.[1] If ever there was a case that called for the review for which higher courts are instituted, this was surely one. Yet such review was effectively prevented by a barrage of dubious

---

[1] One does not expect perfect candor or a nice regard for truth in lawyers' briefs, and it is, therefore, not surprising to find the counsel for the complainant denying the public fact that Russell had been a teacher for most of his life, in England and China as well as in the United States. But one is taken aback to find gentlemen who are members of the Board of Higher Education telling the Appellate Division that "the post of Professor of Philosophy at City College is a brand-new position. It never existed previously and was never held by any prior incumbent. Indeed, the Department of Philosophy itself is a new department created by the Board in 1940." The fact which any reader can verify is that the Department of Philosophy has existed at the City College almost from its beginning. In my own lifetime Professors Newcomb, McNulty, Overstreet, and myself were officially designated as professors of philosophy. Can this have been unknown to Mr. Tuttle, who has been a member of the Board for more than thirty years and for a long time chairman of the Administrative Committee of the City College? It is rather the Department of Psychology, an offshoot of that of Philosophy, that was first established in 1940. And it was the post of Professor of Psychology, to which Dr. Murphy was appointed, that was then created. Russell was to fill the chair left vacant by Professor Overstreet's retirement. Acting President Mead in recommending Russell also mentioned the position still unfilled since my own retirement early in 1938.

It is also, I confess, hard to believe in the sincerity of these gentlemen's concern about Russell's acquiring permanent tenure after a year's service, when they knew that the whole term of Russell's service could not, because of the legal age limit, be more than a year and a half. Strange, how men zealous for public morality will so often be disdainful of honest truth in their arguments!

technicalities. That such a thing can happen in a great American city is an ominous indication of how precarious are the constitutional rights of "due process" which are often supposed to go back to Magna Charta.

Let us look at the main facts of the record.

Bertrand Russell was, on the recommendation of its Philosophy Department and of its Acting President, regularly appointed Professor of Philosophy at the City College and thereupon resigned his previous professorship at the University of California in Los Angeles. Soon thereafter a public clamor was raised by Bishop Manning (supported by various non-educational bodies) that Russell's appointment should be rescinded, i.e., in plain English, that he should be dismissed, because of his views on religion and morals. Against this proposal Russell's fellow-teachers of philosophy throughout the country, and all the educational authorities of the institutions with which Russell had been connected, publicly protested and endorsed his qualifications. The Board of Higher Education then voted to stand by its original appointment.

The next day a complaint was brought in Judge McGeehan's court in Manhattan in the name of a Mrs. Kay of Brooklyn, asking that Russell's appointment be declared illegal because he was not a citizen and not a man of moral character. No evidence was brought to sustain the latter charge except the submission of several volumes of Russell's writings, published some years ago. The Corporation Counsel appeared on behalf of the Board of Higher Education (through an assistant, Mr. Bucci) and contended that the complaint should be dismissed. Mr. Bucci properly offered no evidence in refutation of the complaint, since proper judicial procedure required that the court first rule on his motion to dismiss the complaint as a legally insufficient

[135]

cause of action. Within two days Judge McGeehan announced his decision disqualifying Russell in language which clearly showed the heat of a biased or partisan pleader eager to convict rather than the careful judgment of a responsible judge who has, in conformity with the duty of his office, conscientiously considered the rights of both sides of the case. There were also a number of statements in his written opinions which are simply not true. Thus he said that "the Court had witnesses" [note the plural] "produced in court." The record shows this statement to be categorically false. No witnesses appeared in court. Mrs. Kay merely swore that she was the petitioner, on the judge's assurance to the Corporation Counsel that this was merely "so that her name will appear in the record." No one claimed that Mrs. Kay was a competent witness to testify as to Professor Russell's fitness for the position of professor. Nor can we accept as true the statement of the judge that the respondent "informed the Court that he would not serve an answer." Mr. Bucci denied it in a sworn affidavit which was never challenged. It was confirmed by a sworn affidavit by Mr. Fraenkel,[2] who at no time was given a chance to produce evidence refuting the scurrilous and defamatory statements in the complaint and in the judge's written opinion. Judge McGeehan's reference to the proceedings as a trial has no support in fact or law. He pronounced judgment on Russell on the supposed ground of having read some of his books, but without asking Russell whether the views which he (the judge) read into these books were really there and if so whether Russell still adhered to those views.

Let us now consider the three alleged legal grounds for declaring Russell's appointment illegal.

The first point was that an alien may not teach in a New

York college. The statute invoked clearly refers to public schools that are directed to hold Arbor Day and other exercises that no one supposes to be obligatory in a college. It provides that teachers shall be graduates of normal schools and hold licenses, which no college professor is ever required to do. Even in the public schools the law allows an alien to teach if he declares his intention to become a citizen. Professor Russell had at least ten months in which to do so before qualifying for the active performance of his duties. Judge McGeehan tried to disregard this clear provision of the law by the arbitrary guess that the Federal courts would bar Russell from citizenship. If there were any real basis for this guess the opponents of Russell would surely have tried to have him deported on the ground that a person of moral turpitude was not qualified to enter this country. But Judge McGeehan's mind was obviously not on the law. He himself declared that he would be writing for the legislature as well as the Court of Appeals, and it is not unfair to suspect that he also had in mind the daily newspapers. This is shown by his final appeal to a narrow local prejudice in the argument that "other universities and colleges both public and private seem to be able to find American citizens to employ." As an argument this is clearly worthless in law as well as in logic. Any implication that our institutions of higher learning do not employ foreign scholars is patently false. Long lists can readily be compiled of foreign teachers in municipal and state institutions as well as in private Catholic, Protestant, and Jewish colleges. In New York City not only the city colleges, New York and Columbia Universities, but the institution which Judge McGeehan himself attended have gladly availed themselves of the opportunity when a distinguished foreign scholar was available. This has long been considered an honored practice in New York as in other

[137]

States. The laws of the United States have recognized its national advantage and have exempted such foreign teachers from the usual immigration quotas. To deprive our students of the best available teachers would obviously be to impoverish our country intellectually. Only petty ward politicians, ignorant of the essentially international character of all science and philosophy that seeks the truth, can ignore this. In any case, we surely have an issue here that should not be settled by the arbitrary whim of a judge of first instance who gave barely two days to the hearing of the case and to the writing of his opinion. Surely this should receive the careful consideration of the highest appellate courts.

The second ground on which Russell's appointment was declared illegal was even more unprecedented and revolutionary in its implication. It is that a professor in any public college in New York State must take a civil service examination (by whom?). This is a view so contrary to the experience of our institutions of higher learning that it is hard to believe that anyone in the smallest degree acquainted with the practices of modern colleges can in good faith maintain it. If this ground of the decision in the Russell case were sound law, every one of the professors in every one of our State-supported colleges would have to be dismissed and every member of the Boards of Trustees or Higher Education be penalized for the illegal appointments. Also the Commissioner of Education of the State of New York would have to be punished for permitting so many to teach in violation of the law. The truth is that not even all the teachers in the public schools of New York State outside of two large cities are required to take examinations at all. The law clearly provides that examinations shall be held only when practicable, and the educational authorities in touch with actual conditions have never found examinations practicable in the appointment of professors in institutions of higher learning. Yet Judge McGeehan blandly asserts that the assumption by the Board of Higher Education that competitive examinations were impracticable was "unwarranted, arbitrary, and capricious." One might with more justice apply these epithets to the judge's own decision.

The third ground of the decision is of fateful significance not only to the independence of our educational system but for the general conception of the judicial function. That an individual judge may, on the basis of reading a number of passages in a scholar's works, set up his own judgment as to whether the author is fit for a professorship in a college, and venture to overrule the faculty and the educational authorities to whom such determination is expressly delegated by law and who have had more opportunity to study and competently to interpret these works, is a strange and ominous legal doctrine. Judges are not supposed to be endowed with superhuman wisdom or omniscience in all matters. They are therefore generally restricted to pass only on the question: What has the law provided? Hence it has always been regarded as a sound and established legal principle that, where discretion is expressly conferred on administrative officials, no judge may interfere by simply setting up his own judgment as to the wisdom of what an administrative body did. He may act only if there can be no reasonable doubt that the administrators had gone beyond the power granted them. That this cannot possibly be so here is evidenced by the fact that almost all qualified educational authorities who expressed themselves in the case, including hundreds of American teachers of philosophy, regarded Professor Russell as eminently fit and urged the Board of Higher Education not to revoke his appointment.

The Western Philosophical Association, after the decision

[139]

in the Russell case was announced, unanimously adopted a resolution which in effect insisted that teachers of philosophy (as of other subjects) should be selected on the advice of those competent in their special field and not by judges after listening to arguments of lawyers. (What distinguished scholar will want to accept a professorship if thereby he subjects himself to having his name besmirched in a litigation in which he has not even a chance to appear in court to clear himself?) And Chancellor Chase of New York University won the reluctant approval even of the *New York Times* (which had been rather hostile to Russell) when he urged that, no matter how much one may disagree with Russell's views, the question whether a judge may overrule educational authority in passing on the fitness of a teacher (on the basis of the latter's *opinions*) had not been properly settled and needed to be reviewed by the higher courts.

The statement that the appointment of Professor Russell "is in effect establishing a chair of indecency" is a rather scurrilous way of referring to the several hundred eminent teachers of philosophy who endorsed his appointment and to the Universities of Chicago and California, and Harvard, where he had served as professor of philosophy to the expressed satisfaction of students, fellow-teachers, and educational administrators. One had a right to expect that a court of law pronouncing judgment as to the possible influence of a certain teacher would take into account the testimony of actual pupils as distinguished as Dr. Marjorie Nicolson, Dean of Smith College (where Russell had lectured) and President of the national association of the United Chapters of Phi Beta Kappa. Dr. Nicolson had been a pupil of Bertrand Russell at the British Institute of Philosophical Studies and wrote that both in a large popular course and in a small seminar "Mr. Russell never introduced into his dis-

[140]

cussions of philosophy any of the controversial questions which his opponents have raised. . . . Mr. Russell is first and foremost a philosopher, and in his teaching he always remembers that. I should have had no way of knowing Mr. Russell's opinions on marriage, divorce, theism, or atheism, had they not been given an exaggerated form in the newspapers."

Judge McGeehan condemned Russell as an immoral person because of his divorce record in England. This record was known to the authorities of the many colleges, including those for women and the co-educational ones, where Russell was invited to teach and gave a course of lectures. In a country where many leaders of our public life have been divorced, can it be said as a matter of law that teachers who have gone through such marital difficulties must be dismissed? [3] Many, perhaps a majority, of our people regard George Eliot as one of the noblest women of the nineteenth century, though she lived in what was legally an adulterous relation with George Henry Lewes.

It is not necessary to point out to any literate audience how forced and utterly unwarranted is the misinterpretation of Russell's writings adduced in justification of the monstrous charge that Russell's appointment would endanger the health and morals of New York through his inciting young people to masturbation or to the crimes of homosexuality and abduction. But the tolerance and even favorable

---

[3] In this connection it is curious to note that while Judge McGeehan was District Attorney of Bronx County a large number of divorces were there granted on legally sufficient evidence of adultery. But though adultery is a crime in New York State, District Attorney McGeehan never prosecuted a single one of the parties whose guilt was thus officially recorded.

One is reminded of the story of the lady who congratulated Dr. Johnson on having left out all obscene words from his dictionary. "Madam," said the honest doctor, "I am sorry you looked for them."

comment which Judge McGeehan's rhetorical opinion received in parts of our public press show how urgent it is that those who know anything about the history and importance of freedom of thought should keep the public informed as to the necessity of the distinction between incitement to crime and the free expression of philosophic doubt as to the adequacy of our traditional or conventional morality. In defending society against crime we must not suppress the questioning mind, which has been the basis not only of democratic but of all liberal civilization, as distinguished from societies of robots that act either from habit or according to what others tell them.

Judge McGeehan himself publicly expressed his expectation that his decision would be appealed and reviewed by the higher courts. What prevented the important issue which he raised from receiving due consideration from any of our higher courts? The first obstacle was the technical ruling (unfortunately sustained by our Court of Appeals) that Mr. Russell could not be made a party in a suit in which his reputation and his position as a teacher were at stake. This is marvelously strange when we consider the interest of Mrs. Kay in the suit. None of her children could possibly have been able to take any of Russell's courses at the City College. In the first place they lived in Brooklyn, and if they went to college at all they would naturally go to Brooklyn College rather than to the City College, which is in upper Manhattan. In the second place her daughters could not be admitted to the City College, which in its regular classes does not admit women. And in the third place, as Russell would have to retire in 1942 because of the age limit, none of her children could possibly have managed to qualify for admission in Russell's classes. If she were really interested in keeping her children from contact with Russell's

[142]

ideas she should have applied for an order restraining publishers from publishing Russell's books, booksellers from selling them, and public libraries from circulating them; for in fact Russell has had far more popular influence through his writings than through his classes, which have always been highly technical. I think it is important to bear in mind the fictitious character of Mrs. Kay's interest which the courts were so eager to protect that they refused to let Mr. Russell answer her complaint. The reason given was that she was suing the Board of Higher Education and should not, therefore, be compelled to litigate with Professor Russell, though in fact she was trying to deprive him of the right to pursue his calling, on which he and his children depended for their living. If this is law, then surely in the language of Dickens "the law is an ass."

An honest friend of the venerable doctrine of "due process" might have expected that it would operate against depriving a man of his property and reputation without ever giving him a chance to be heard. But such expectation would also have shown serious innocence as to the forces behind the scenes in this case.

Very significant is the part played in this unsavory case by the Corporation Counsel of New York City. At first he appeared (through his assistant, Mr. Bucci) as counsel for the Board of Higher Education and contended that there was no justification in law for the removal of Professor Russell from the position to which he had been appointed. But after Judge McGeehan's decision he not only refused to vindicate the law by appealing the case but actively and effectively opposed the effort of the Board to do so.

What reason did he give for this radical change of attitude? Clearly not that the judge's written opinion convinced him that the office of the Corporation Counsel had been mistaken as to the law in the case. On the contrary, in his letter to the Board of Higher Education he quite definitely intimated that Judge McGeehan's decision was not in conformity with the law. The reason alleged for his "advice" was a rather thinly veiled opinion that the higher courts could not in this case be trusted to decide the issues involved on their merits. He therefore urged the Board to obey a decision unwarranted by the law and break a contract entered into in good faith by both parties, thereby committing a horrible injustice on Professor Russell, who had resigned his previous position in California in reliance on the honor and official action of the Board of Higher Education in New York City.

It is, frankly, hard to believe that an honorable legal official of a great municipality could thus be willing to participate in a grossly dishonorable (if not illegal) procedure, if he were not under some pressure not referred to in his letter to the Board. And indeed there is some evidence of intervention by the Mayor, who gave the identical advice to the Board. Two incidents point in this direction. The first is the haste of the Mayor in putting into the city budget a provision that no part of the money of the Board of Higher Education should be used to pay Russell's salary. This was an unprecedented move of no real legal force, for if anything is established in the Education Law of New York it is the complete freedom of a school board to control expenditures within its own budget. Certainly the Mayor and the Board of Estimate have no right to interfere in the appointment of a professor in our city colleges, nor have they the right to bring about the removal of anyone who has been appointed. The action of the Mayor was just "a play to the gallery" for political reasons, just as was the action of the City Council.

[144]

The second indication is the Mayor's subsequent action in publicly directing the Corporation Counsel not to appeal a case where the Board of Education was involved. Now a city, like any other client, may instruct its counsel not to appeal a case if such appeal will not serve its best interests. But where an agency such as a Board of Education has by law been granted certain powers, with which the Mayor cannot interfere, then his preventing an appeal hamstrings by indirection that which he may not directly control. No Mayor will openly tell the Board of Higher Education to appoint Professor X or to dismiss Professor Y. Yet to prevent the college from using its funds to pay a given teacher is to all intents and purposes compelling it to discharge that teacher. The Mayor has not been provided with facilities and the law certainly gives him no power to deal thus with the employees of our educational institutions. But whatever the influence of the Mayor, there is no doubt that an effective judicial review of the issues raised by Judge McGeehan's decision was prevented (1) by the Corporation Counsel's refusal to appeal from an order the granting of which he had opposed on good legal grounds, and (2) by the Appellate Division sustaining his power to prohibit the Board of Higher Education from appearing in court through any other lawyer. This extraordinary situation, by which an administrative body is prevented from defending in court the legality of the acts within its province, was sustained by the Appellate Division in an argument which, to say the least, begs the whole question. That court said: "There is no duty resting upon the Board to engage the services of Russell." But since this court refused to consider the merits of the contention that Russell's original appointment was illegal, the *prima facie* contract between the Board and Professor Rus-

[145]

sell could not be thus set aside. Even an Appellate Division cannot abrogate a contract while at the same time it refuses to consider the question.

Despite all technicalities, no one can deny the obvious fact that by a solemn official act the Board appointed Professor Russell and that he in reliance thereon gave up another position. In the minds of all honorable men, therefore, the Board of Higher Education incurred a contractual obligation to disregard which would be disgraceful to the fair name of any city.

Even more important is the larger significance of the unlimited power thus given to the Corporation Counsel. For by preventing the Board of Higher Education from appearing in court to defend what it regards as the proper interpretation of its duties, the Corporation Counsel thus becomes not its legal servant but its master, and this subjects it to all sorts of abuses without its having any legal recourse. The cherished independence of the educational system of New York from political interference, which has been built up through the years and has been recognized by the highest courts,[4] is thus completely destroyed. This is an ominous and sinister situation. The office of the Corporation Counsel is instituted so that the city and its various departments may have adequate legal advice and have their rights defended in the courts. The Corporation Counsel is a lawyer. He may advise his clients that they have a bad case in law, or perhaps even that they are likely to lose a good case because of his suspicion that the judges of last resort are prejudiced and will not decide according to the law. It may even be argued that he has a right to express his opinion that the Board of

---

[4] "If there be one public policy well established in this State it is that public education shall be beyond control by municipalities and politics." —Chief Judge Crane in *Matter of Divisich v. Marshall*, 281 N. Y. 170, 22 N. E. (2) 327 (1939).

Higher Education would be wasting the city's money in litigating a given case. But this was not the situation in the Russell case, where the members of the Board of Higher Education, anxious to deal honorably with Professor Russell and to carry to the Court of Appeals the grave issues involved, generously agreed to pay for counsel at their own personal expense. But in any case, there is no sound reason of public policy why the Corporation Counsel should be able, by his own arbitrary opinion, to prevent important issues from receiving the full consideration for which our courts are instituted.

THE ATTITUDE OF
THE EPISCOPAL CHURCH

By Guy Emery Shipler

The Attitude of
the Episcopal Church

No aspect of the Bertrand Russell case has been more widely misunderstood than that which has to do with the attitude of church people toward the important questions it has raised. It has been widely taken for granted that almost all church people thoroughly approved the assault on Dr. Russell following his appointment to the teaching staff of the College of the City of New York and that they got no small elation out of the witch hunt. When the serious opposition to Dr. Russell began with an attack by the Rt. Rev. William T. Manning, Bishop of the diocese of New York of the Protestant Episcopal Church, it seemed to be assumed by the public not only that the bishop was speaking officially for his own church but that his point of view was that of most churchmen of all denominations. The facts deny both assumptions.

Because a few communions are authoritarian in their form of government it seems to be the illusion of the public in general that all Christian denominations fall into this category, whereas Protestantism, with rare exceptions, operates under a thoroughly democratic form of government. Certainly that is true of the Protestant Episcopal Church of which Bishop Manning and I are members and in the government of which laymen have an authority equal to that of

[1 5 1]

bishops and other clergy. In spite of this fact, when Bishop Manning burst into the public prints with his vitriolic denunciation of Dr. Russell and his appointment, it was stated in more than one editorial and news story that the bishop spoke "as a representative of the Protestant Episcopal Church" and the public assumed that this statement was correct. The error was due, no doubt, to ignorance concerning the democratic form of government characteristic of the Episcopal Church and, equally, to the added assumption that a bishop of a metropolitan diocese as large as that of New York must have some sort of mystical authority not possessed even by other bishops of his church.

Hoping to overcome somewhat the misapprehension, I pointed out in the *New Republic* that "Bishop Manning has been given no authority to represent the Protestant Episcopal Church in such controversies," adding: "He is one voice, and only one, out of a million and a half communicants. He has every right to speak for himself; he has no right to speak either for his own diocese or for the national church. He cannot speak even for the episcopate, of which he is one among 153. No authority has been given him to represent either the House of Bishops or his diocesan convention in this matter. Only the General Convention, composed of bishops and other clergy and laymen, could authorize him to speak for the Episcopal Church. It is unfortunate that the public is under the illusion that every time a bishop, particularly a bishop of a metropolitan diocese, bursts into print with a point of view stemming from the Dark Ages he represents the Protestant Episcopal Church."

I am not pretending to intimate that there are not millions of people in the Protestant churches who agree with Bishop Manning's point of view concerning the Russell case, but it is highly important to emphasize that there are also millions who thoroughly disagree with him. In other words, opinion in the Protestant churches would, if an honest poll could be taken, probably be found as varied as opinion outside the membership of those and other churches. And incidentally, it might well be remembered that Protestant churches in the United States are not given to interfering with public educational procedure.

These facts, it seems to me, are of fundamental importance. As long as Americans go on assuming that all Protestantism in this country is represented by authoritarian individual voices, as too many did in this case, enlightenment in the social order will go on suffering a quite unjustifiable slowing down.

There is also, concerning Bishop Manning's activity in this case, an equation to which I have seen little reference in public, but which, for reasons that will be obvious, ought to be emphasized. It will be recalled that Justice John E. McGeehan wrote an opinion denouncing Professor Russell chiefly on moral grounds. The general point of view of the opinion reflected fairly closely that which had been expressed by Bishop Manning. It is well known, of course, that Justice McGeehan is a Roman Catholic and that he received his education in Roman Catholic schools. It is not so well known, outside the Episcopal Church, that Bishop Manning is an Anglo-Catholic, that is, one of the comparatively small group in the Episcopal Church whose theological concepts and whose concepts in the field of "morals"—speaking technically—are essentially identical with the official standards of the Roman Catholic Church. The Anglo-Catholics—formerly called High Churchmen—resent the appellation of "Protestant" and are therefore irked because the official title of their church in this country is the *Protestant* Episcopal Church. They have made numerous efforts to have the

[153]

name of the church changed to the "American Catholic Church" or some other title which would eliminate the hated word. They have always failed in spite of skillfully organized campaigns, owing to the fact that the great majority of Episcopalians glory in what they conceive to be the Protestant character of their church, though they also cherish the word "Catholic" when it is used in its original and unrestricted sense.

All this may seem beside the point, but it ought to be remembered that the persecutions of teachers and other leaders of thought throughout the ages have emanated from those holding such fixed ecclesiastical concepts as those represented by Justice McGeehan and Bishop Manning. The same dogmatic attitude is found, of course, among fundamentalists in the Protestant churches.

The question as to whether one agrees or not with Professor Russell in the field of "morals" seems to me quite irrelevant in this discussion and I have not, therefore, touched on it. I should think that it had nothing whatsoever to do with the question of teaching mathematics. If it does, then we ought to be logical and fully adopt Hitler's revival of medieval witch hunts and torture.

The furor reminded me of an amusing story told in his *Autobiography* by William Lyon Phelps. In a kind of reverse, it is an apt commentary on the Russell case. Mr. Phelps was once approached by Miss M. Carey Thomas, president of Bryn Mawr College, with the suggestion that he might become a member of her teaching staff. In the course of her conversation she inquired: "What are your views on religion?" to which Mr. Phelps replied, "I am a Christian and a member of an evangelical church." Mr. Phelps continues the record as follows: "To my amazement, a look of intense disappointment, almost of horror, came

[154]

over her face. 'I am deeply distressed to hear this. I am most anxious that our girls be left with entirely free and open minds. I do not want them unduly influenced by religious doctrines or biased by any theological or superstitious views. This is a serious drawback, Mr. Phelps. Do you think that you could keep your religious prejudices out of the classroom?' I replied that I understood that I was hired as a teacher of English, and not as an evangelist."

Those of us who are liberals in the various churches are glad to have Bishop Manning and all others proclaim and defend their points of view as effectively as possible; that is the kind of democratic procedure for which we shout lustily. (And one recognizes that a few who call themselves liberals opposed the appointment of Mr. Russell.) But we do get fed up with the public assumption that pronouncements from reactionary sources represent either the official or the majority opinion of church people or both. It is false to assert, as so many have done, that the churches opposed the appointment of Bertrand Russell. It is no truer than it would be to assert that the United States opposed his appointment.

THE CASE AS A
SCHOOL ADMINISTRATOR
SEES IT

By Carleton Washburne

The Case as a
School Administrator Sees It

THINGS which, in moderation, are essential, may be
fatal when excessive—like hydrochloric acid in the
stomach. Public control of education is of this nature. So,
too, is academic freedom. The Bertrand Russell case places
the issue squarely before us.

One extreme, which is one horn of the dilemma, would
be the employment in an educational institution of a staff that
is utterly repugnant to the parents of the young people who
are to be educated thereby. If Bertrand Russell, for example,
were really a writer of materials which were "lecherous,
salacious, libidinous, lustful, venerous, erotomaniac, aphrodisiac, atheistic, irreverent, narrow-minded, untruthful, and
bereft of moral fiber," who condoned homosexuality, was a
sophist and quibbler, all of whose alleged doctrines "are just
cheap, tawdry, worn out, patched up fetishes and propositions, devises for the purpose of misleading people," as
charged by Attorney Joseph Goldstein—if such were the fact
and the administration of any educational institution insisted on employing people of this type on its faculty, the result would be fatal to that institution. An executive head who
persistently made such appointments would not be retained
by the Board of Trustees. If he were, the trustees would be
replaced if there were any way of replacing them. If they

[159]

were completely independent and self-perpetuating, the parents and schools which sent students to the institution would cease to do so. In any case, if the policy were not changed the institution would go out of existence.

The other horn of the dilemma is equally obvious: if we have an extreme of direct public control of education the schools and colleges will be mere reflections of the opinions of an uninformed majority of the mass. Instead of making for progress, they will impede progress; instead of promulgating truth, they will perpetuate misconceptions, prejudices, and superstitions. The teacher who has a new point of view, or has made or is aware of a new scientific discovery as yet unpalatable to the majority who know little or nothing about it, will not be able to work toward informing future majorities, will be unable to contribute to the advancement of thought—he either will not be employed or he will be dismissed.

Since it is impossible for the general public to be informed on all matters with which each specialist deals, the majority opinion is bound to be a prejudiced and uninformed opinion. If teaching is to reflect only such opinion, no truly educational institution can exist. Again, excess is fatal.

The resolution of the dilemma lies in the avoidance of excesses in either direction. It is difficult or impossible to find examples of institutions which go to the first extreme—that of employing and retaining a considerable number of teachers who in their utterances and their personal lives give unbridled expression to opinions and attitudes which are highly repugnant to a majority of those whose children they are to teach. The fatality of this excess is so obvious to teachers, administrators, and trustees that it does not occur. Individual excesses, however, may occur at times. Protected, or hoping to be protected, in his academic freedom, an oc-

[160]

casional professor may exercise what he conceives to be his right to complete independence of expression, to advocate, in class and out, his opinion on a hotly controversial question, regardless of consequences to his institution. He is not always willing, however, to take the consequences himself.

Should he limit himself, or be limited? The strongest advocates of academic freedom are likely to answer No. Such absolutism, however, is theoretical, not realistic. As a *reductio ad absurdum*, think of trying to retain on any faculty teachers who openly advocated homosexuality—or the assassination of the President. The degree of realizable academic freedom is inversely proportionate to the degree of public intolerance—the intensity and extensiveness of the public's repugnance to a particular type of expression will, regardless of theory, affect the freedom of such expression.

The teacher who is wise recognizes this as a fact, and adjusts himself to it without going to the opposite extreme. The adjustment, actually made by most teachers, including many of the most courageous and most unorthodox, does not involve the suppression of facts; but it places more faith in them than in opinion and exhortation.

The wise teacher recognizes that it is better education to let students draw their own conclusions from well-organized facts than to impose his conclusions upon them. He will insist upon the right of the students to all the facts which are available and pertinent. But he will use judgment and an understanding of social psychology in the manner of his expression, in the degree to which he expresses, in school or out, his personal opinions, and in the degree to which he allows his personal life to depart from accepted *mores*.

This limitation applies to people in all walks of life— the doctor, lawyer, architect, businessman, laborer, farmer, housewife. When one is a part of a society one has to reckon

[1 6 1]

with the concepts and feelings of that society. One can, in a civilized culture, depart in many ways a considerable distance from the norm without seriously harmful consequences to oneself and with advantageous consequences to social growth. But there is always a limit. The teacher who thinks that this limit does not apply to him is not facing reality.

The administrator must necessarily take this fact into account in employing and retaining faculty members. He must recognize that neither students nor the public will segregate a man's teaching in one field from his general teachings, his statements in class from his public pronouncements, his philosophy from his life. He must recognize that, whether or not it ought to be so, students and public consider that the appointment of a teacher places a stamp of approval on him as a whole; it invests him with a prestige which seems to justify youth in considering him an example whom it might be well to follow. The teacher must be considered in his entirety. This does not mean that he must be a plaster saint, but it means that his assets must clearly outweigh his liabilities. A serious failure in judgment as to social psychology may outweigh scholarly assets.

The trustees in turn must select an administrator whose judgment of men and whose judgment of the public are sensitive and wise. He must be able to select faculty members skillfully, to help them understand public reactions, and help the public to understand the faculty. And the trustees themselves must be people in whom both the public and the faculty have confidence as to vision, judgment, fairness, and courage.

By these means the excess of academic freedom can be avoided. But are we not in danger of the opposite extreme —of a faculty chosen because its beliefs coincide with those of the administration, an administration which kowtows to the trustees, trustees who make their institution a mere reflection of uninformed mass opinion?

The danger of going in the direction of this extreme is exhibited in the Bertrand Russell case. Here the fault lay not in the faculty, administration, or trustees, but in the concepts and actions of certain elements of the public. These elements said, in effect: "If the administration and trustees make the mistake of appointing an unsuitable person, why should not the people, through their courts or otherwise, have a right to correct the mistake?" But if that is admitted, don't we get right back to the Scopes-evolution problem in Tennessee? The scientific teaching of evolution was considered by the legislature to be counter to religion and therefore to morals. A teacher of modern biology was therefore repugnant to the people of Tennessee. Had they not the right to refuse to allow him to be employed? And we find ourselves impaled squarely on the first horn of our dilemma with all the consequences of impeding progress and making a travesty of education.

The difficulty lies partly in a misconception of democracy. We confuse direct responsibility to the people with ultimate responsibility. And we fail to recognize the essential role of the expert.

The faith of democracy is that *in the long run* an *informed* majority of the people will reach right decisions. The majority often has to become informed by the painful process of making mistakes. But neither by this process nor any other can the people become informed about everything. Therefore, for most matters they must delegate authority to people who will become expert in certain fields and must give these people the power to act. *Ultimately* the experts are responsible to the electorate, but not directly for each several act. A city manager, for example, is chosen for his

[163]

expertness, and given broad powers. He is removed from direct pressures from the electorate. If as a whole his administration is unsatisfactory, the council replaces him. If it fails to do so, the people elect a new council. This plan usually works. It would be completely disrupted, however, if the people directly or through the courts could interfere with any single legal action of the manager.

More and more we are having to delegate authority to responsible individuals and commissions who are free to act with the minimum of restraint. The cry of "dictator" is sometimes raised when this is done, but it is completely unjustifiable as long as freedom of criticism remains and as long as the people can, indirectly, bring about a change. No amount of power given to the President of the United States, for example, makes him a dictator, in the Fascist sense of the word, if he is subject to free public criticism, to laws passed by the Congress, and to removal at the end of his term of office, and even impeachment.

If a democratic form of government is to be effective, delegation of power to experts, removed from direct political pressure, is essential. Only so can we act in the light of the best available knowledge. Only so can we rise above the dead level of uninformed and prejudiced opinion. Only so can real progress be made.

Somehow we must get this principle across to the people. It is one matter on which they can be and should be informed. There is a possibility of bringing about a general understanding of such a principle, when there is not the possibility of bringing about an understanding of each of the innumerable details of government—or of education. The mistakes that are made by a failure to apply this principle give the people direct experience on which they can base their judgment.

In the conduct of an educational institution this principle must be made to apply—it is the only way to avoid both horns of our dilemma. The teacher must have complete freedom to teach all facts, however impalatable they may be, without fear of dismissal. Beyond this he should have the right to go as far as practicable in the expression of conviction and personal opinion and to be as free as practicable in his personal life. Theoretically, perhaps, he should have utter freedom of expression; but, as we have seen, this is unattainable for him as it is for all other people. The greater the freedom of expression, however, the more truly educational an institution can be. To help the present public, and especially the future public that is now in our schools, to recognize that education and social growth are proportionate to freedom and diversity of expression is the most basic responsibility of educators, administrators, and trustees.

The administration must have freedom to make appointments to the staff. It must assume the responsibility for seeing that people of widely divergent views are included, and must have courage, vision, and tolerance as well as sound judgment. It will be responsible to the faculty, and, while guiding it as to ways of avoiding abuses of academic freedom, must protect its right to promulgate the truth as each member sees it.

At the same time, the administration will necessarily be responsible to the trustees. This responsibility, however, does not mean subservience as to any specific act—the trustees should not exercise or have the right to determine with finality the appointment of a faculty member. They should examine individual appointments or other actions of the administration and be free to counsel in regard to them. But they usurp the function of administration if they interfere with the actual conduct of the institution—they substitute inexpert for expert judgment. The formulations of policies, both fiscal and general, in consultation with the administration, and the selection, retention, or dismissal of the administration are two of their three sole functions. The third is the interpretation of the institution to the public and of the public to the administration. In the latter they may help to keep the staff from unnecessarily and harmfully antagonizing the public, but this influence must be exerted with caution lest it smother the breath of life. In interpreting the institution to the public, on the other hand, there is little danger of going too far. Trustees have no more important responsibility than that of protecting the administration and staff in their freedom of thought and expression and educating the public as to the essential value of this if education is to contribute to progress.

Through this middle way a certain amount of democratic control of education is exerted—and the fatal extreme of a disregard of the public is avoided. At the same time the control is sufficiently general and indirect to allow great freedom to the teacher and consequent progress and enlightenment.

This is no utopian dream. As a matter of fact, it is a picture of the actual situation in many of our best educational institutions—in some public and private schools, in some public colleges and universities, and in many privately endowed institutions of higher learning. And it is effective.

The public, however, has not as yet clearly seen the picture. Our educational institutions have been singularly lax and inept in helping their own students to understand the principles on which schools and colleges must be conducted if they are to be truly educational. The student may learn much about Latin, or physics, or Elizabethan literature, and graduate with no inkling of the problems and principles of

[166]

the institution which is giving him knowledge. He may learn to discuss social problems intelligently, and never have heard of the problems of educational freedom and the wise administration of schools and colleges.

The judge who ruled against Russell, the lawyer who prepared the vitriolic indictment of him, the mayor who refused to let the corporation counsel appeal the case, the bishop who damned him, the people who upheld the bishop, were all products of our educational institutions. If we are to have public support for the diversity of views, the freedom of expression, and the type of administration which alone can enable our schools and colleges to be forces for education and progress, these very institutions must take the responsibility for helping their students to an intelligent understanding of the role of the expert in the government of a free society and of the necessity for giving students access to all facts and to the widest possible diversity of opinions and convictions. Our students must leave our schools with not only such an understanding but with a determination to protect freedom of thought and expression. Only so can we avoid cases analogous to that of Bertrand Russell. Only so can our schools and colleges be educational institutions.

THE COLLEGE,
THE COMMUNITY,
AND THE
BERTRAND RUSSELL CASE

*By the Philosophy Department
of City College*[1]

[1] The authors of the essay are Daniel J. Bronstein, Abraham Edel, Lewis Feuer, Yervant H. Krikorian, Joseph Ratner, Philip P. Wiener, which group includes all the members of the Department during 1940, the year of Professor Russell's appointment.

The College, the Community, and the Bertrand Russell Case

I

IN recommending the appointment of Professor Bertrand Russell and throughout the controversy that arose thereafter, the Department of Philosophy of the City College was guided by certain principles concerning the nature of teaching and the place of the college in a democratic community. The City College is a tax-supported institution in New York City. The taxpayers, in the widest and fairest sense of the term, are the people of New York. The college serves the needs of the community by providing higher education for those young people who are able and willing to acquire it. This education is free and open to all, irrespective of race, religion, political belief, economic status, and country of origin. In its long history, the college has served this purpose well. Its general influence in the community has been a progressive one.

Not all groups in the community have favored the work of the college. There have been some who have resented the fact that it was educating the children of workers and of the lower middle class, that it was giving opportunities to immigrant groups and thus helping them toward full equality in American society. For some elements, the college has

[171]

always been an undesirable extension of democracy and social equality. As a consequence it has not been expanded as rapidly as the community's needs required. The various groups opposing the college have shown themselves ready to attack it on the slightest pretext and have waged constant warfare against its good name. The Russell case is a dramatic and portentous episode in the history of the college.

Our conception of the obligations and responsibilities of the teacher at the City College is guided by our view of the reciprocal relations between higher education and the life of the community: the college has to meet the educational needs of the community, it has to transmit the enduring values of culture, and it has to clarify the purposes and increase the scope of the democratic ideal toward which enlightened mankind has been painfully striving. Only by keeping firmly and clearly in mind the various functions of a liberal college can there be developed satisfactory criteria for deciding, then, to what degree and in what respects it is desirable for the college to be responsive to the majority opinion of the community. History provides ample evidence that progress and the general welfare of mankind are best served by freedom of inquiry. Academic freedom is not freedom from communal responsibility but an instrument for fulfilling that responsibility.

Unless the college enjoys the right to explore possibilities, higher education cannot contribute to progress but will be a definite hindrance and obstacle. The gap between what is taught in college and what is going on in the community will be widened. The students on graduation will not be prepared for adult participation in the life of the community. To restrict college education to the inculcating of ideas and attitudes that will support the *status quo* at all costs is in fact to constrain the college to supporting the past.

There is another consideration which is almost always completely neglected in popular movements that have as their objective making the college "safe." Most people, not excluding educators, tend to be conformists. No elaborate precautions are needed, nor special pressures and inducements, to make the overwhelming majority of educators, in private as well as in public institutions, feel and think in terms of the dominant social pattern. They will do that anyway. What is sorely needed is adequate support and encouragement for the few who exhibit intellectual courage and originality. The practice of rewarding the inventor and the discoverer in the technical scientific and technological fields has contributed greatly to the enrichment of American material culture. American spiritual culture will be as greatly benefited by rewarding creative minds in social fields. It is our firm belief that it is essential for democracy that such minds enjoy the right to work and teach in publicly supported educational institutions.

The common purpose of enlightened teaching in all fields is to stimulate reflection, to develop independent thought on the part of the student. This is especially true of the function of philosophy. To help the student understand the ideas of others and to clarify his own, to help him systematize his thoughts and achieve some consistency of belief, is the essential educational objective of philosophy, both within the college and without. In the educative process the principal function of the teacher of philosophy is to act as a catalytic agent. It is not his function to impose a set of ideas upon the student, but to present alternative points of view and to discuss them fairly. This process, when successfully carried out, develops in the student both intellectual self-reliance and the dissociation of ideas from personalities. Thus the teacher is enabled to preserve his individuality and present his

[173]

unique contribution without running the danger of indoctrinating his students.

The essential qualities for a teacher are fair-mindedness, intellectual honesty, the ability to understand and formulate views contrary to his own, imaginativeness, analytic power. These qualities are neither dependent upon nor necessarily correlated with any specific dogmas, whether of religion, politics, economics, or morals. The removal of religious and political tests for educators is a cornerstone of the free democratic education in America, and remains fundamental to the preservation of social freedom and progress.

These general principles are the foundations of the democratic faith. The Board of Higher Education in 1938 gave them fuller realization through the reorganization of the college's administrative structure. This reorganization gave the teaching staff a new and enhanced role in all functions of the college—in the formulation of educational policy, in reaching decisions concerning educational standards, and in selecting the teaching personnel. The effect on the individual teacher has been to widen his scope and deepen his sense of responsibility. The teacher has become an increasingly effective part of the college, co-operating with his fellow-teachers and administrators in working out the purposes of the institution in and for the community.

II

The Russell case is significant because it involves these basic principles. When Professor Morris Raphael Cohen and Professor Harry Allen Overstreet retired from City College, it was agreed both by the Philosophy Department and by the administrative authorities of the college that the addition of an outstanding philosopher to the staff would be

[174]

highly desirable. Mindful of the statement made on one occasion by the Chairman of the Board of Higher Education —"Nothing is too good for City College"—the department, after carefully considering the available professors of philosophy throughout the learned world, recommended that an invitation be extended to Professor Bertrand Russell, one of the most eminent of living philosophers. The college authorities and the Board of Higher Education unanimously and enthusiastically accepted the recommendation. In the words of one member of the Board, it was the "educational scoop" of the year. Professor Russell was eagerly sought by many American universities of high standing. He had taught at the University of Chicago, was teaching at the University of California at Los Angeles, and was scheduled for the William James Lectures at Harvard. Our chief concern had been that he might not find an offer from City College sufficiently attractive. Following the Board meeting of February 26, 1940, Acting President Nelson P. Mead issued a statement to the press to the effect that the college was singularly fortunate in being able to secure the services of a man of such international reputation and distinction as Bertrand Russell.

The department and the administration were surprised and shocked at the character and vehemence of the attacks which certain groups immediately launched against Professor Russell's appointment. From Bishop Manning's first pronouncement to Justice McGeehan's decision, the attacks seemed to us to be based on a conception of the educational process in colleges and universities that is contrary to the fundamental principles of education in a democracy.

The main charge directed against Professor Russell by Bishop Manning was that Russell was morally incompetent to be a teacher of youth. The Bishop asked: ". . . What is to be said of colleges and universities which hold up before our youth as a responsible teacher of philosophy and as an example of light and leading a man who is a recognized propagandist against both religion and morality, and who specifically defends adultery . . . ?" In support of his public query, he cited disconnected passages from a few of Russell's books dealing with sex and religion. And in Justice McGeehan's decision the consideration of Russell's moral fitness played a decisive part.

The Justice was on firm ground when he stated that ". . . the personality of the teacher has *more* to do with forming a student's opinion than many syllogisms," [2] and also when he stated that the more eminent the teacher, the greater his influence is likely to be on impressionable and developing minds. "It is contended that Bertrand Russell is extraordinary. That makes him the more dangerous."

However, the Justice's evaluation of Professor Russell's character is, in our opinion, wholly erroneous. The influence of Russell's character would be beneficial not only to the students but also to the whole college and through the college to the community. For we cannot conceive how it could be detrimental to anyone to be exposed to Russell's qualities of intellectual and moral courage, to his integrity, his uncompromising devotion to truth, his profound concern for the advancement of human welfare, his tolerance in all provinces of human thought and action, his love of freedom, his disinterestedness and unselfish maintenance of principles. It is our belief that these qualities make Professor Russell eminently desirable as a teacher, not merely of logic and the philosophy of mathematics but also of ethics.

It is evident that, in the attacks of Bishop Manning and Justice McGeehan, the objection to Professor Russell on

---

[2] Italics ours.

moral grounds has its source in a basic opposition to freedom of thought in general and to academic freedom in particular. Any thinker who stimulates people to reflect critically over fundamental human questions is "dangerous." In this sense Professor Russell is truly a "dangerous" man. As Mrs. Russell pointed out felicitously in a letter to the editor of the *Journal of Social Studies,* a student publication at City College, "To them [groups opposing Professor Russell] argument itself is impious. It is not so much my husband's actual opinions they object to as his belief that ethics is a subject for argument, that it is for human beings to discover by thought and experiment what rules of conduct and what social institutions will do most to promote human welfare in any given age, and that morality is made for man and not man for morality."

III

The opponents of Professor Russell were consciously and unconsciously advocating that a publicly supported educational institution should teach one specific ethical-religious doctrine. This, in essence, is sectarianism in education and would inevitably lead to the introduction of religious tests for appointment to public colleges. We need hardly point out that such a development would subvert the basic law of the land. The separation of church and state, and its consequence, the elimination of religious tests for public or civil service offices, are among the great historical achievements of the Constitution of the United States. It is essential to the continuance of American culture that students be given not only the opportunity but the intellectual training necessary for examining different conceptions about man and society. Only in this way can independent self-reliant minds

[177]

be developed. Only in this way can the rising generation grow into ethical maturity.

The strength of the movement to override the traditional American separation of church and state is evidenced in the recent legislation in New York State permitting time off from school for sectarian religious instruction. It is also evidenced in the widespread attempt in the domain of general social theory to base political democracy on an exclusively religious foundation. It is true that the religious emphasis on the dignity of man has historically been an important factor in developing the democratic outlook. However, it is important for an understanding and preservation of our traditional liberalism to recognize that the democratic idea can be firmly and effectively established on a non-religious basis. This is implicit in the practical separation of church and state established by the Constitution. And in the realm of philosophic theory there are several different systems which furnish a non-religious basis for the whole of liberal thought and action.

IV

The McGeehan decision not only crystallized the views and attitudes of those who opposed Professor Russell's appointment, but in some respects went much further. The decision is particularly dangerous to academic freedom and to public higher education.

The central and novel contention of the McGeehan decision would, if carried out literally, make a criminal of every critical-minded person. In a statement to the Bertrand Russell–Academic Freedom Committee which was read before the Board of Higher Education, Professor Arthur O. Lovejoy, former President of the American Association of

University Professors, and of the American Philosophical Association, wrote:

The gravest feature of Justice McGeehan's decision consists in the assumption which he makes in order thus to bring the case within the scope of the criminal law. That assumption is that *the expression of an opinion that an existing legal prohibition is ill-advised and socially undesirable is to be judicially construed as an incitement to other persons to violate the law, and therefore as itself unlawful.* Thus Justice McGeehan declares Mr. Russell "not fit to teach in any of the schools of this land" on the ground that "he encourages the violation of the Penal Law of the State of New York"; and in his second opinion Justice McGeehan states, as the final and most decisive of the "ultimate facts" justifying the original decision, that Mr. Russell "does not deny that he has expressed opinions in conflict with existing penal laws which he characterizes in his proposed answer as 'antiquated' and 'in need of revision.'" No evidence is cited that Mr. Russell has in fact ever incited anyone to break any law of the State of New York or of the United States; it is simply assumed that criticism of the ethical premises underlying certain laws is *eo ipso* an incitement to break them. This principle, generally applied, would be destructive of liberty of speech and of the press; for it implies that any advocacy of alterations in, e.g., the criminal law is an encouragement to crime, and consequently criminal.

There is in fact no limit to which such "logic" may be carried. If criticism of present standards of sexual morality is incitement to adultery, then criticism of present property arrangements is incitement to theft, criticism of a cigarette tax incitement to smuggling, criticism of an existent poll-tax incitement to insurrection, and criticism of any matter on which the criminal law directly or indirectly touches can be turned into incitement to illegality. Such a "legal doctrine" is potentially a weapon against academic freedom. It can be used by any elements of a community that regard

[179]

a mere whisper of change, or the least criticism of existing arrangements, as a threat to "law and order."

A second issue of major importance which the McGeehan decision raised is the relation of the courts to administrative bodies established by legislative act. In effect, the justice assumed the right of the court to nullify the law which expressly gave to the Board of Higher Education the power of appointment. On this phase the *Herald Tribune* wrote an incisive editorial which said in part: "If it were sustained the net of the decision would seem to be that any Supreme Court justice could cancel any City College appointment (and could he not, on these same grounds, cancel any appointment to any private institution, for that matter?) if he happened to find anything in the candidate's past record which led the justice to think that his teachings might tend to encourage his students to any violation of any penal law." The *New York Post* said editorially: "The issue becomes one of whether the Board of Higher Education controls City College, or whether any one of the several dozen justices of the Supreme Court can set himself up as a super-Board of Higher Education and veto the acts of duly constituted authorities in the field."

Such assumption of right on the part of the court in relation to an administrative agency having the powers of appointment and policy-formation is particularly inimical to the democratic process. With the creation of federal administrative bodies, which is an increasing phase of the development of American life, this issue has become one of far-reaching national importance.

There are a number of other special issues raised by the McGeehan decision; for example, at a time when America was becoming host to an increasing number of refugee scholars, the Justice's ruling would deprive the City Col-

[180]

lege of the opportunity to make appointments of aliens. It also jeopardized the very positions and tenure rights of the college staffs.

V

The triumph of those who opposed Professor Russell's appointment was an encroachment of the demagogic process on the democratic process. The demagogic process depends for its success upon making mass appeals to blind prejudice and on combining divergent and contradictory issues in one cohesive confusion. The democratic process, on the other hand, seeks its objectives by enlightenment and by clarification of issues.

The twofold technique of the demagogic process is clearly exhibited in the activities of Professor Russell's attackers. They began by charging Professor Russell with immorality and atheism—accusations which are most potent in arousing unthinking passions. Then the anti-alien element was introduced, then the charge of communism, then pacificism, then political comments which Professor Russell allegedly had made during the first World War. The charge of immorality and atheism remained throughout the controversy the center of attack; it functioned as the basic social glue which gave a semblance of coherence to the additional arguments advanced for annulling Professor Russell's appointment. One of the most frequently used epithets was "barnyard morality." Justice McGeehan's judicial decision followed the popular standards of expression and mode of analysis. He denounced the appointment as "an insult to the people of the City of New York"; he reached the threshold of fame with his dictum that the appointment was equivalent to creating a "chair of indecency."

The treatment accorded Bertrand Russell is not an iso-

[181]

lated or accidental case. It is important for the defenders of academic freedom and the advancement of American life to recognize this. The opponents do. They were quick to use the Russell case as a breach through which to press forward toward their more comprehensive objectives. Very rapidly the attack was broadened to include the Board of Higher Education, which had established a reputation for progressive reforms. From that point on, nothing of liberal or progressive practices and ideas in college education has been immune from assault. A resolution was introduced into the State Legislature calling for a sweeping investigation of the educational system; the outcome of this legislative interest was the Coudert subcommittee of the Rapp-Coudert Committee.

In its widest significance, the Russell case—like the condemnation of Socrates, the inquisition of Galileo, the Scopes trial, and many other comparable cases—is a symbol of the everlasting struggle for the freedom of the human mind. Professor Russell pointed this out in his reply to the editorial suggestion of the *New York Times* that he should have resigned his post as soon as the opposition acquired momentum. As he wrote in part:

But however wise such action might have been from a personal point of view, it would also, in my judgment, have been cowardly and selfish. A great many people who realized that their own interests and the principles of toleration and free speech were at stake were anxious from the first to continue the controversy. If I had retired I should have robbed them of their *casus belli* and tacitly assented to the proposition that substantial groups shall be allowed to drive out of public office individuals whose opinions, race, or nationality they find repugnant. This to me would appear immoral.

It was my grandfather who brought about the repeal of the English Test and Corporation Acts, which barred from public office anyone not a member of the Church of England, of which he himself was a member, and one of my earliest and most important memories is of a deputation of Methodists and Wesleyans coming to cheer outside his window on the fiftieth anniversary of this repeal, although the largest single group affected was Catholic.

I do not believe that the controversy is harmful on general grounds. It is not controversy and open differences that endanger democracy. On the contrary, these are its greatest safeguards. It is an essential part of democracy that substantial groups, even majorities, should extend toleration to dissentient groups, however small and however much their sentiments may be outraged.

In a democracy it is necessary that people should learn to endure having their sentiments outraged.

All through the public controversy City College was never alone in its defense of academic freedom. The vigor and spontaneity with which liberals all over the nation rallied to the cause of intellectual freedom was a heartening demonstration of the vitality of democratic ideals in the United States.

We cannot name all the individuals and organizations who took part in this defense. Among them were college and university presidents and deans, leading educators, faculty members of our own as well as of other colleges, scientists and liberal theologians, publishers, columnists, newspapers, labor unions, parents' organizations, teachers' organizations. The student bodies, in particular at City College and the University of California at Los Angeles, added their invaluable support. It is especially gratifying that a large number of the members of the American Philosophical Association and its Western Division, which was meeting

[183]

at the time, came to the support of our common professional ideals.

To all individuals and organizations who joined us in defending democratic ideals in education we take this opportunity of expressing our deep appreciation.

THE GENERAL PATTERN

By Sidney Hook

The General Pattern

THE very existence of this volume is evidence that the case of Bertrand Russell concerns others besides himself. His cause is their cause, since it involves the integrity of the teaching profession and the principles of free inquiry. But the case of Bertrand Russell concerns not only his colleagues; it concerns every American parent and citizen as well, for it portends a grave cultural trend in American life whose shadow, apparent today in many quarters of the land, may become substance tomorrow.

The cultural trend of which I speak is definitely related to the momentous changes that are taking place in the underlying economic and social structures of our age. The economy of the free market in goods and services is gone beyond any recall. The crucial question for us is: Can a free market in ideas still be preserved, and perhaps extended, within the framework of the social and economic order slowly emerging before our eyes? In almost every other country in which the free market has disappeared, we have witnessed, together with the sharp rise in state powers and controls in the production of goods, ruthless monopolistic controls of intellectual and cultural life. These controls, formally invoked in the name of all, are in fact exercised to consolidate the power of some special group or interest. Is this destined to be the pattern of American cultural life?

The issue has not yet been decided. There is no compelling reason to believe that the irreversible movement which is producing a national economy under growing state control necessarily entails the disappearance of our cultural and civil freedoms. We know by the evidence of history that however incompatible an economy may be with certain cultural patterns, it is at least compatible with more than one. Consequently, what American cultural life shall be in quality and principle will not depend *exclusively* upon the character of today's or tomorrow's economy. For this reason the culture of our America presents us with a set of challenges in a field in which our choices, our judgments, our actions can still influence the future. Our responsibilities are limited only by our opportunities.

In what follows I shall give an account of some of the pressures and pressure groups which are making for cultural uniformity and totalitarianism in America, particularly with reference to education. In the nature of things no exhaustive analysis can here be presented, for the details of the picture are changing daily. But the account will be sufficiently definite to enable us to identify the chief tendencies in the cultural life of the nation toward which American democrats must be "At alert!"

I

Freedom in education, like all freedom of inquiry, involves a critical evaluation of attitudes, knowledge, and techniques. Despite widespread claims to the contrary, the processes of criticism, in their proper function, do not terminate in negativism, wholesale skepticism, and systematic disbelief. For one thing, we can be intelligently skeptical about something only if we are not skeptical about something else, viz., the evidence which justifies the initial skepticism. And far from resulting in general disbelief, criticism often provides us with grounds for better and more warranted belief. No piece of knowledge which recommends itself to us as true, no value which seeks to enlist the support of intelligent and generous-spirited men, need therefore fear the processes of criticism. It is the merit of democracy as a way of life, social, political, and personal, that, distinct from any of its rivals, it can welcome and withstand criticism. Whoever seeks to choke off criticism because on occasion it may lead to a rejection of a cherished myth or congenial fallacy betrays an irresoluteness or uncertainty, often overlaid by truculence, about his own articles of belief or objects of allegiance.

A chronic source of opposition to critical currents in American education and culture is the reactionary pressure groups. Among these, the most conspicuous are companies of super-nationalists and some business associations. The first act as if they hold an exclusive organizational patent on the term "patriotism." They often seek to substitute themselves for law-enforcement agencies, and thus subvert the democratic American traditions they allegedly wish to sustain. They have no independent program but can always be procured by certain religious and economic groups to join a crusade against this or that progressive and liberal cause. The height of their virulence was reached soon after the first World War, but with the passing years their influence, if not their articulateness, has declined.

Much more efficacious are the business associations. Businessmen have become increasingly aware of the fact that the trends of economic change since 1929 have to a large extent shaken their social status, their prestige with the public, and their influence upon the government. More often than not, they attribute this shift of their ground and worth to attitudes developed in consequence of direct instruction in the nation's schools. What more natural than that they should judge the adequacy and effectiveness of our schools in terms of the evaluations they make of business enterprise, the free market, government "encroachments" upon industry, and all the customary shibboleths of the age's business *mores?* The organized review of the nation's textbooks, under the auspices of the National Association of Manufacturers, the periodic campaign against liberal education by the notorious New York State Economic Council, are eloquent signs both of the suspicion of businessmen that something not to their liking just must be going on in the schools, and of their determination to do something about it, regardless of whether it is going on or not. The fact that they are more heavily represented on the school boards throughout the country than men of any other interest puts their fear of the schools in a particularly ironic light, but it reveals them in an exceptionally strategic position with regard to the patterns of American education.

That textbooks, curricular studies, methods and materials of teaching must suit the requirements set by any group, except the group consisting of competent educators themselves, is a notion that runs counter to any intellectually honest, democratic educational system. After all, what special group, except that of the experts trained for the purpose, can with any right presume to decide what is *educationally* sound for all groups? Why businessmen rather than workers, or farmers, or government officials? Why should a book be read to see if proper deference has been paid to the profit motive rather than to civil liberties or the living conditions of the plain people of the land? If an occupational group relies on well-qualified professional superi-

[190]

ority in its own special business, would it not be the part of logic and wisdom to rely upon the same necessary qualities in education? Those qualities are special skills in seeking and communicating truth. But no pressure group which seeks to impose its will on the schools will admit that it wants to communicate something else than the truth. It will not say more even when it means more. And by this attitude it unconsciously acknowledges that the function of the school and of the teachers is to discover as much of the truth as they can see. Once men have agreed that they want schools in the community, and that the task of the schools is to help create personalities rich and well developed in body and mind, they have also committed themselves to the faith that the teaching professions can develop their own standards of competence and integrity in their educational quest. The relevance of this commitment to the astounding treatment of Bertrand Russell by the Mayor and the courts of the City of New York need not be elaborated on.

The concern of the businessman with the schools of America, in so far as it is not the concern of a father for his child but of an occupational interest for its special and invidious advantage, is a symbol of his failure to understand the world he is living in and in which his child must grow up. For the future role and final destiny of business enterprise will not, and cannot, be determined by what is taught in schools. These are being determined by what is happening on the battlefields of Europe, the workshops of industry, the halls and offices of government. Only the schools can be free to illuminate those dark events with knowledge; in this way they may help save present values for future times.

The old economic order passes. No schoolroom paeans of praise to businessmen can arrest the passage. The main question is, once again: Can we on the basis of a new economic order, which business itself is blindly establishing, build a cultural life in which ideas can develop freely, subject only to the restrictions of scientific method and rules of evidence? Do we have enough faith in *intelligence* to leave the defense of truth, human decency, and morality in its hands rather than in the hands of self-appointed custodians of the public good?

Already this basic problem is beginning to be posed in acute form in American education today because of the stresses and strains of converting the nation into an arsenal of international democracy. Within the rules of the democratic process there is always room, in war as in peace, for a legitimate opposition. It may plausibly be argued that such a legitimate and loyal opposition, i.e., one which abides by the method and spirit of democracy, justifies itself even from the viewpoint of practical results in furthering national objectives. It is sometimes true that treasonable elements which owe allegiance to foreign powers seek to cloak themselves as a wing of legitimate opposition. Such efforts of course must be exposed. But it is no less true that near-sighted partisanship and selfish, vested interests often attempt to discredit or silence legitimate opposition by maligning it as a form of treason. The first step in such a direction usually takes the form of intolerance toward expressed criticism of popular attitudes and beliefs. That is why a positive appreciation of the role of criticism in education, in schools and out, is of the first importance in a healthy democracy.

II

We turn now to another highly organized pressure group whose influence has been increasingly felt in American culture and education.

[192]

(a) Some months ago a community forum in New London, Connecticut, invited Bertrand Russell to speak on a philosophical theme. He accepted the invitation. As soon as his lecture was announced, the director of the forum received a visit from the local Catholic priest. The purpose of the visit was to demand that the invitation to Mr. Russell be recalled. Should it not be recalled, the priest threatened, the Catholic Church would withdraw from the interfaith program in which it had been participating, quite amicably, up to that time. After some hesitation the forum canceled Mr. Russell's lecture.

(b) In the fall of 1940, the Massachusetts Mothers' Health Council wrote to the Rev. Ronald J. Tamblyn of the First Congregational Church of Holyoke, Massachusetts, requesting permission to use the church building for a talk by Mrs. Margaret Sanger on behalf of "fundamental civil liberties in the matter of birth control." The meeting was to be a plea for support of an initiative petition to the State Assembly urging a change in the existing law whose provisions forbade even qualified physicians to give birth-control information to married persons. The Standing Committee of the church authorized the use of its building for the meeting. Shortly thereafter, the Rt. Rev. Msgr. John F. Fagan of St. Jerome's Church, "ranking leader of Roman Catholicism in Holyoke," issued a statement which was read at masses denouncing those who were sponsoring Mrs. Sanger's lecture on the initiative petition. Prominent businessmen, who were members of the First Congregational Church, were visited by Msgr. Fagan and others. A day before the meeting the Standing Committee was hurriedly convened at a special meeting and, over the opposition of Rev. Tamblyn, voted to rescind the permission for the Margaret Sanger meeting "in view of the emergency created by the

Catholic opposition." Officially the action was explained as having been taken "for the sake of community harmony," but one of the members of the Standing Committee subsequently declared:

The primary discussion of the Church Committee at its meeting on Wednesday, Oct. 16, revolved around the following questions: first, consideration of the right of the Church Committee to continue in an action that might have weighed economically on other members of the congregation who had no opportunity to participate in the official vote of the Committee; secondly, the possibility of a disturbance at the meeting; third, the future of the Church and its members at Holyoke. . . . It was in an atmosphere of concern for the economic well-being of members of the Church congregation that the Committee finally took its action.[1]

In effect, the Catholic Church had used the club of an economic boycott to compel the First Congregational Church of Holyoke to cancel a meeting held to petition for a change in the law.

(c) About a year ago Father William C. Kernan, priest of the Protestant Episcopal Church, was invited by a lodge of a Jewish fraternal order, the B'nai B'rith, to make an address under its auspices. Father Kernan is known as an outspoken critic of Coughlinism. The *Tablet* of Brooklyn, New York, organ of the largest Catholic diocese in the world, printed on page one, under Hearst-like headlines, "Protest against Propagandist," a letter addressed by Rev. Joseph E. McLaughlin, pastor of the Parish of Our Lady Queen of Martyrs, to this lodge of the B'nai B'rith. The letter said, in part:

---

[1] All quotations, and details, from "Information Service of Department of Research and Education," Federal Council of the Churches of Christ in America, Vol. 20, No. 12, March 22, 1941.

In the interest of preserving these happy, peaceful relations, I urge upon you the necessity of canceling the proposed address. In the face of this protest, should this peaceful community be torn asunder by racial or religious strife in which friend is set against friend, and neighbor against neighbor as the result of the introduction by new arrivals into our community of an element of discord and dissension such as this proposed address represents, I now, as a matter of public record, put the responsibility where it belongs—with the B'nai B'rith. *Neither I nor my people will be responsible for any reprisals of a social, financial, racial, or religious character which are likely to occur* as the result of the action of the B'nai B'rith, for I am now indicating publicly where the responsibility belongs.[2]

(d) Some time ago the Rapp-Coudert Committee, designated by the legislature of the State of New York to investigate subversive activities in the New York City public school system, presented evidence at a public hearing that several members of the staff of the municipal Brooklyn College were members of the Communist Party and had participated in its political activities. Whereupon Rev. Robert I. Gannon, the Jesuit head of the largest Catholic college in the East, declared: "It might be well that as subversive political policies in our educational programs are being investigated today, we also investigate the subversive philosophical policies in these same programs." [3] His own distinction indicates that he is referring not merely to Communist political doctrine but to philosophical conceptions like naturalism, which, leading Catholics hold, is guilty together with all forms of non-Catholic philosophy of subverting the foundations of moral and social order.

(e) Before the year was out in which Bertrand Russell

[2] *Tablet*, March 9, 1940, p. 1. My italics. S. H.
[3] *New York Times*, December 7, 1940.

had been deprived of his post, there were signs that those who led the campaign against him had become emboldened by their success. In the fall of 1940 Dr. Gardner Williams, of the faculty of the University of Toledo, delivered a paper on "The Nature of Ultimate Moral Authority" before the Northwestern Ohio Philosophical Society at Findlay College, in which he defended the principle of ethical relativity —a philosophical position which extends at least as far back as Protagoras and which has been developed by some of the great figures in classical and modern philosophy. Whereupon the *Catholic Chronicle,* official newspaper of the diocese of Toledo, launched a vigorous attack on Dr. Williams, demanding that the University of Toledo dismiss him, since these philosophical views proved that he "whitewashes sin" and "blacks out God." The *Chronicle* admitted that Dr. Williams "has a perfect right to think whatever he pleases," but then added that "thinking as he does, he has no right to remain on the faculty of tax-supported University of Toledo." Since all universities are directly or indirectly tax-supported, the same demand can be made against any professor whose philosophy runs counter to Catholic dogma or to Catholic interpretation of natural law.

These incidents have been selected almost at random. They could be multiplied many times over. They are representative of a powerful and dangerous current in American educational life, the most dramatic expression of which is the Bertrand Russell case. The success of the campaign against Russell means that no American scholar and educator, whose views do not conform to those of fundamentalist censors of whatever creed, is safe from public calumny, from persecution, from loss of his livelihood. Secularism in education, established with great pains by the democratic

[196]

working men and women of our land, is on the defensive throughout the country. Unless a determined and organized effort is undertaken to resist the systematic attacks against it, the traditional separation of church from state, so characteristic of our national culture, will be undermined. And with it the principles of free public education will be nullified.

The spearpoint of the offensive against the separation of church and state in the United States is the Catholic Church. For a number of reasons, plain speaking about the role of the Catholic Church in public and political affairs is discouraged. Not least among the reasons is the manner in which even the gentlest criticism is received by the Church, whose representatives have not been sparing of the most scathing pronouncements against others. Just as the Communist Party seeks to silence any critic of its philosophy and program with the cry, "Red-baiting!" so many Catholic dignitaries wail, "Bigotry!" as a reply to any criticism, no matter how sweetly reasonable, of their political ways. *Here I wish to state as explicitly as I know how that criticism of some Catholic practices, and of certain Catholic attitudes toward the cultural problems of American life, does not imply in the slightest any opposition to the religious freedom of Catholics or any other religious group, including Jehovah's Witnesses.* The truth is that the Catholic Church, far from being under attack by liberals in this country, is in the van of today's attack, all along the line, against the best liberal traditions of American culture and education. These traditions were developed within the historical setting of diverse religious loyalties and in consonance with the American ideal of democracy. During the last century religion was definitely recognized as a "private matter." Legal provisions were

[197]

made to protect the community as a whole from being subjected to either doctrinal domination or financial exploitation by any religious group.

The revival of a movement which may culminate in the introduction of sectarian religious controls into American education is obviously a very ominous threat to the separation of the church and state in America. In many instances the exploratory efforts of this movement have already succeeded, and it is an interesting observation that in many quarters the successes are due to the skillful way in which certain fears of the American public have been capitalized and played upon. These fears are directly connected with the triumphs of Hitlerism and their dire consequences for us. A widespread and subtle campaign is afoot to persuade the American people that the basic values and attitudes of our democratic way of life may not be able to withstand the attacks of totalitarianism, from without and within, unless they are fortified by supernatural sanctions.

Those who entertain such a sentiment overlook the fact that many countries with powerful and authoritative religious organizations and public religious education have found them to present not the slightest obstacle to the march of Fascism. In some countries, indeed, totalitarian movements have grown up around religious organizations, and their apologists have invoked religious justification for the political programs and activities of Fascist parties. The record of clerical Fascism in Austria, Spain, and Portugal demonstrates the connection. Even if it were true, as it well may be, that certain kinds of religious education could fortify democratic ideas and practices, the historical record puts on liberals the obligation to distinguish in its light between religions which serve to strengthen democracy and religions which do not. But this duty to distinguish and to

[198]

evaluate is precisely what partisans of religious education would avoid, saying that it is divisive and productive of disunities.

Grant that religious education, on no matter what creedal basis, can truly help in grounding and justifying an intelligent democratic philosophy of life. Does it therefore need to be introduced into the public schools, after it had been separated from the schools for cause? Religious instruction can be given by private religious agencies without robbing the public school of time for the purpose. Further, there is a danger that emphasis upon creedal differences will exacerbate, rather than harmonize, existing religious differences. If the creedal elements be eliminated from religious instruction, then what remains as the least common denominator of the major religions in our land is certain broad ethical principles which are already employed in the secular training which forms character. This training can be extended and strengthened without departing from our characteristic American principles of free public democratic education.

If unity among believers in a democratic culture is desirable—and unity may take other forms than uniformity —then only the strengthening and defense of concrete democratic practices can serve as the rallying point, not allegedly "basic principles" of theology or metaphysics. For many official spokesmen of the Catholic Church have voiced "basic principles" which, taken seriously, would make impossible a united front with non-Catholic opponents of Fascism. According to these spokesmen, the root of the cultural decline of the West is to be found in the philosophy of paganism, whose technical expression is positivism. They characterize the Protestant Reformation as the historic occasion for the insurgence of paganism and positivism in modern Europe. They allege that one line of development leads by gradual but necessary steps from Protestantism to Fascism and Bolshevism, from Luther to Hitler and Stalin. That such allegations are demonstrably false is not their worst feature. Most disturbing is the fact that if Catholic action were to be based upon them tolerance of religious differences would come to an abrupt end. The democratic community would be rent with irreconcilable conflicts at the very moment when the maximum of uncoerced unity and faith in democratic procedure is required to defeat Fascism, whatever its color, red, black, or brown.

On many occasions Catholic spokesmen express themselves in a fashion which makes their participation in interfaith activities difficult to understand except as a strategic method of propagating the true faith. Just as members of the Communist Party profess a belief in the Bill of Rights until such time as they come to power, when the Bill of Rights will be denied to non-Communists, so authoritative Catholics invoke an appeal for religious tolerance now, until such time as they come to power, when tolerance of religious heresy will cease. Were America ever to become a Catholic state, say Fathers Ryan and Boland, in their *Catholic Principles of Politics*, "It could not permit non-Catholic sects to carry on general propaganda nor accord their organizations certain privileges that had formerly been extended to all religious corporations, for example, exemption from taxation" (p. 320). Although the event of its practical realization is admitted to be remote, the authors insist that the principle none the less "is very true in logic and theory," and that their church cannot surrender it.

One cannot escape the impression that it is with an uneasy mind and divided heart that the Catholic Church looks on the limited forms of co-operation with other religious groups. The interests of organizational survival impel the Church to defend itself against possible totalitarian repression. Fear of the consequences of common democratic activity on its hierarchical and non-democratic structure; hope that a *modus vivendi* may be worked out with whatever wave of the future may succeed in washing democracy away; the implications of policy in its own doctrines of revealed and absolute truth—all tend to pull ecclesiastical Catholicism out of the orbit of co-operation with non-Catholic faiths. The faithful watchdog of Catholic organizational interest is the Jesuit order. And it is in the Jesuit publications, which constitute the largest and most influential section of the Catholic press, that voice is given to these reflections. The Rev. Leslie Rumble, writing in the Jesuit magazine *America,* delivers himself of the following, whose vein can be matched by many similar pronouncements:

I must confess that I have little confidence in the Protestant churches as allies in the fight against paganism. . . . If it be urged that this is no time for controversy, and that we should forget our differences in order to unite as far as possible in a common fight against the inroads of paganism, the disturbing thought comes that Protestantism has really proved the ally of paganism. Have not Protestant ministers contributed to the undermining of the Gospels? . . . In themselves, all forms of Protestantism are unjustified. They should not exist.[4]

I do not mean to suggest that there is a unanimity of sentiment and belief on these matters among Catholics in America. There are a number of distinguished liberal figures in the Church, and a few Catholic publications have spoken up in criticism of the reactionary tendencies described above. But they find themselves isolated and with

---

[4] *America,* January 4, 1941.

little influence. Hierarchical support goes not to the weak liberal elements within the Church but to their opponents. Often liberal Catholics who plead for a more tolerant spirit toward American fellow-citizens, who urge stronger opposition to Hitler and Mussolini, and who do not give unqualified support to the Franco regime, are subjected to vicious attacks in Catholic publications. The situation within the Catholic Church is described in vivid detail by an outstanding Catholic educator and liberal, Dr. George N. Shuster, President of Hunter College of the City of New York. He points out quite truly that "the great majority of [American] Catholics, like the great majority of their American fellow-citizens, have always been opposed to Hitler." But he also attests that "an influential group was for a long time persuaded the German leader had been grossly maligned and that the Church would suffer no loss of prestige or opportunity if it refrained from 'political' activity."

The opposition between the liberal and reactionary tendencies within Catholicism, according to Dr. Shuster, was international. Speaking of Germany, he writes: "Catholic men and women who had offered heroic resistance to Hitler were suddenly astonished to find their ecclesiastical superiors not merely eager to compromise but actually willing to believe Nazism a benign affair. The members of the Catholic majority in the legislative assembly of one federal state were startled to behold, as they were marched out of jail by their Nazi captors, their Archbishop riding down the street in an automobile festooned with swastikas and giving the Nazi salute."

But of more direct concern to us is the situation in America. The same influential, strategically situated minority carried matters whenever an issue appeared: "Catholic journalists who wrote in criticism of what was happening in Germany were often targets for abuse. Insulting and threatening letters accused them of economic dependence on Jews. I repeat that the number of those involved was small; but it was a determined, violent, and influential minority. Thus, when an attempt was made to stop American participation in the Berlin Olympic Games, the anti-Hitler forces failed to carry the day because Catholic support was withdrawn at the critical moment. A few prominent pro-Nazis gained the victory." He further asserts that "a very considerable number of Catholic journals have been tinged with anti-Semitism."

Dr. Shuster makes it quite plain that the tendency represented by Father Coughlin and the *Tablet* has no support from liberal Catholic intellectuals. But just as plain is it that these intellectuals are not in a position to affect in any vital way Catholic policy. For, as Dr. Shuster says, "Unfortunately the influence of these intellectuals is decidedly limited. On the one hand, they are without status inside their own communion. On the other, they get precious little support outside it. The writer of Catholic books can find no market; and the instructor in the Catholic college has no tenure." [5]

III

From an unexpected source powerful support comes to the movement for the religious reorientation of education. In the writings and position of President Hutchins and Professor Mortimer Adler, both of the University of Chicago, we read a plea for a revolutionary transformation of the basis of all modern education. The details appear to have

---

[5] All quotations are from Dr. George N. Shuster's article, "The Conflict among Catholics," *American Scholar*, winter 1940–41.

been worked out only for institutions of higher learning. There, metaphysics and theology are not to be, as they are now, elective courses for students interested in taking them. They are to be *prescribed* for all students in institutions of higher learning and given primary place in the hierarchy of studies on the ground that the truths of metaphysics and religion are "superior" to all other truths, particularly to those reached by scientific method.

The fact that many who have been influenced by these doctrines do not see their drift, and that President Hutchins is happily unaware of the implications of his views for academic freedom, does not detract from the importance of these doctrines as cultural portents. For it can easily be established that repressive practices in both school and society logically follow from them and are justified by them (which accounts in part for the cordial reception their doctrines have received in the Catholic press). Let us see why.

According to Messrs. Hutchins and Adler ethics and politics are "superior," i.e., more rational, sciences as compared to any of the natural or experimental sciences. The basic truths of ethics and politics depend upon a metaphysical insight which is direct, immediate, and *certain*. In so far as moral values imply a reference to the supernatural order and revelation, and in some respects it is asserted that they do, they are subordinate to the truths of sacred theology. Consequently, both on metaphysical and theological grounds, there can be only one right set of principles, one right order of goods and values. This one right order, it must be remembered, is not something to be discovered; it is something already absolutely known. Therefore, different and conflicting conceptions of this order are necessarily errors—errors which must lead, and have led, to the corruption of minds and the weakening of the foundations of public order. Now we do not tolerate the deliberate circulation of disease germs which kill men's bodies—and this in fields in which we have only probable knowledge or mere opinion. How, then, can we tolerate the circulation of errors that destroy men's souls and the fabric of Christian culture—fields in which we are fortified by absolute knowledge? Differences on matters about which we have absolute knowledge must be heresies. Heresies of this kind in politics and ethics must be harmful. If public calamity is to be avoided, the heresies must therefore be liquidated. Mr. Adler tells us: "When Christianity loses its active dislike of heresy, it loses its dignity as a revealed religion and becomes no better than one among the warring creeds, as it was in the Hellenistic period" (*Art and Prudence*, p. 300). In a recent address, Mr. Adler has made it clear that the species of Christianism which he favors must hold a place in modern culture similar to the one it held in medieval culture; i.e., it should not take its chances in the equal competition of doctrines, scientific, metaphysical, or religious, but "must be accorded the supreme place in the cultural hierarchy." In the same address, he calls for the liquidation of professorial heresy. If Hitlerism is the only way the root heresy of our culture can be destroyed, he professes his readiness to accept Hitlerism as the sword wielded by the hands of an avenging Providence.[6]

IV

It would be a mistake to assume that the only danger to freedom of teaching and research in education emanates

---

[6] "God and the Professors," an address delivered at the Jewish Theological Seminary, New York City, September 10, 1940. Reprinted in *Science, Philosophy and Religion: A Symposium*, New York, 1941, pp. 120–38.

from chauvinistic associations, reactionary business circles, and dogmatic Catholic quarters. The last, it is true, are more articulate and aggressive, particularly in the East, than other organized agencies. They have the virtue of posing the issue of cultural freedom squarely and do not often resort to subterfuge in proclaiming what limits they would impose on it. If it seems that we are giving them disproportionate emphasis, this is due to the openness and frequency of their stands against democratic educational theory and practice. But any group which claims to be in possession of a special method of reaching truths, a method that can be properly wielded only in virtue of a special faith and organizational allegiance, carries a threat to freedom of education at its heart. At the present juncture of events in America, it may appear perhaps far-fetched to include the totalitarian Communist movement as a unit in the general pattern of reaction. Whoever believes that such an inclusion is far-fetched is pathetically in error. For despite the fact that partisans of Communist totalitarianism are here and there writhing under the lamp of a publicity their past actions have turned on them, the Stalinist party is among the most influential of the totalitarian groups in the secular, cultural life of our country. With a very competent organization, ample resources, and a membership buoyed up by a religious faith which will not scruple at any action, the Stalinists are deeply intrenched in schools, journals, and publishing houses; in the theater, the cinema, and in unions of white-collar workers; in the youth movement and the professions, particularly in certain local, state, and Federal services.

After the Stalin-Hitler Pact, the Stalinist totalitarians beat a strategic retreat. They did so by employing in the main the art of protective coloration. Their main forces, however, remain intact, and a shift in the foreign policy of Russia away from Germany and toward the democratic powers will provide them with another opportunity to reach out for cultural hegemony of vast sectors of American life.

In a very curious way, the "philosophic" rationalization of Communist Party domination parallels the justification given by some theologians for the supremacy of their respective creeds. Communist language is less mystical, but if anything the claims of the Communist Party are more sweeping than those of fundamentalist sects. They proclaim that only such as possess a grasp of the "principles of dialectical materialism" can properly understand the natural and social sciences. To this they add the rule that only those who sooner or later are enrolled in the ranks of the Communist Party can attain a proper understanding of the principles of dialectical materialism. It follows at once that only those who sooner or later are enrolled in the Communist Party can enjoy a proper understanding of the problems and results of any discipline. There is, therefore, a "party line" in everything from mathematics to poetry. Membership in the Communist Party is by itself alone not sufficient, however. One must demonstrate "an unexceptionable political line"; i.e., one must never be out of step with the party leadership. Should the leadership or the political decisions of the leadership change, the party line in all the arts and sciences also changes. This is what is meant by the famous slogan of the "Bolshevization of Science." The Pope in the Vatican is infallible on matters of faith (morals and politics) but not (formally, at least) on matters of fact. Stalin in the Kremlin, however, is mightier than the Pope. He is infallible about anything he chooses to make

[207]

a pronouncement on. And Hitler profits by the example of both. His slogan of the "Aryanization of Science" expresses the same "logic," if with less art, with more passion.

The party line is not merely a matter of theoretical piety. It imposes upon those who hold it, through an iron-clad discipline, the injunction to translate the "line" into practice. This means, among other things, the conversion of all cultural organizations into transmission belts of the Communist Party, the exploitation of positions of educational trust for purposes of party propaganda and recruiting, the use of anonymous scurrility and other methods of character defamation against those who stand up against them. Well-meaning but innocent individuals are often duped by the tactical maneuver, which Communist totalitarians have developed into a fine art, of attaching themselves to worthy causes in order to capture strategic posts of power. Before long these causes are invariably compromised by being utilized for political purposes extraneous to them.

It is not the *beliefs* of Communist totalitarians, wrong and fantastic as they are, which are primarily objectionable but their practices. These practices play into the hands of domestic reactionaries just as the practices of the latter often supply partisans of the Communist Party with occasions for misleading agitation. Both thrive by muddying the waters and obscuring the fundamental issues of a free culture. Democratic and responsible education needs to protect itself from all totalitarian groups at all times, even when some of these groups are for the moment arrayed against each other.

More significant than any theoretical justifications offered for the rapid changes in Communist Party policy and action in our country is the fact that the basic allegiance of the American Communist Party is to a foreign power, Rus-

[2 0 8]

sia. Predictions of the behavior of this party, as of every other Communist Party in the world, can only be made on the exclusive basis of the interests and decrees of the Russian rulers. This is decisive in what concerns the kind of culture the Communist Party would set up in the United States or anywhere else.

V

To those who believe we have gone rather far afield in our discussion of the Bertrand Russell case, certain features of that case should be recalled. Bertrand Russell ranks not only among the foremost philosophers of our time; he has earned a place in the history of philosophy of all times. The act against him occurred in the cultural metropolis of the country, under a presumably liberal administration. To his support there rallied a host of distinguished men, professional associations of his colleagues, and numerous committees devoted to cultural and academic freedom—all to no avail. Well-established legal, educational, and administrative principles were openly flouted in the campaign against him. Although the grounds of reason and fair-play were all on his side, he was not permitted to make an official defense of himself against his detractors.

In view of these circumstances, one can hardly regard this case as a passing incident, unfortunate but without special significance. That it could have occurred in the way it did, and when it did, requires explanation. Part of that explanation seems to me to lie in the general pattern of cultural repression, major expressions of which have been considered above. Whether in the period before us this pattern is to grow stronger, until it ultimately prevails, is a question every whit as urgent for thinking Americans as any

[209]

problem that faces us at present. If the question yields to none in urgency, it takes precedence over all in the momentous consequences of how the decision will fall.

The case of Bertrand Russell is a telling sign that there is no ground for optimism. The gallant defense the case has evoked is just as eloquent an indication that there is no reason for despair. The issue has been joined. The battle for a free American culture, at the home front as well as at our frontiers, is on.

APPENDIXES

APPENDIX I

Decision of Justice McGeehan

In the matter of the application of JEAN KAY, petitioner, v.
   BOARD OF HIGHER EDUCATION OF THE
   CITY OF NEW YORK, respondent, for an order reviewing the determination of the respondent herein, appointing one Dr. Bertrand Russell as Professor of Philosophy in
   the College of the City of New York, and directing the
   respondent to rescind and revoke the said appointment of
   the said Dr. Bertrand Russell.

Decided March 30, 1940.

JOSEPH GOLDSTEIN for petitioner.
WILLIAM C. CHANLER, corporation counsel
NICHOLAS BUCCI, (assistant corporation
counsel, of counsel), for respondent.

McGEEHAN, J.—In this application, under Article 78 of
the Civil Practice Act, the petitioner seeks to review the action
of the Board of Higher Education in appointing Bertrand Russell to the chair of philosophy at City College. Petitioner contends
that the action of the Board of Higher Education was illegal
and an abuse of such powers as the Board of Higher Education
had in making such appointments, because (a) Bertrand Russell
was not a citizen and had not declared his intention to become
a citizen; (b) the appointment did not comply with Article V,
Subdivision 6, of the Constitution of the State of New York with
reference to appointments in civil service on the basis of merit
and fitness; and finally, (c) because the appointment was against

[213]

public policy because of the teachings of Bertrand Russell and his immoral character.

The corporation counsel, appearing on behalf of the Board of Higher Education of the City of New York, moved to dismiss the petition upon the ground that it did not state facts sufficient to constitute a cause of action. The corporation counsel's motion was based solely upon the ground that the provisions in the Education Law with respect to citizenship were not binding on the Board of Higher Education.

Three organizations appeared through their attorneys and asked leave to file briefs as *amici curiae* in support of the appointment of Bertrand Russell. Permission was granted on the argument for the filing of these briefs as *amici curiae*. These three parties contend that the appointment is lawful, that citizenship was not an issue, and the appointment should not be disturbed because it would be an interference with "academic freedom."

The motion of the corporation counsel to dismiss the petition upon the ground that the Board of Higher Education is not required to employ citizens is denied. It is not necessary to pass upon this question to deny the application because the application is based on two additional grounds to which the motion of the corporation counsel was not addressed. The court has afforded the respondent an opportunity to interpose an answer, but the respondent has declined to interpose an answer though counsel has informed the court that its defense is to be limited to the question of law raised by the cross-motion to dismiss the petition.

Petitioner contends, in the first place, that Section 550 of the Education Law requires that "No person shall be employed or authorized to teach in the public schools of the state who is . . . 3. Not a citizen; the provisions of this subdivision shall not apply, however, to an alien teacher now or hereafter employed, provided such teacher shall make due application to become a citizen and thereafter within the time prescribed by law shall become a citizen." It is conceded that Bertrand Russell is not a citizen and that he has not applied to become a citizen. The cor-

[2 1 4]

poration counsel contends that he has a reasonable time after appointment to make the application. He further contends that the section does not apply to teachers in the colleges of the City of New York, contending that if Section 550 did apply, most of the teachers in the colleges of the City of New York would be holding their appointments illegally because they are neither graduates of a state normal school nor have they licenses from the commissioner of education. The section does not require that they have a license from the commissioner of education. It requires in Subdivision 2 that they must either be in possession of a Teacher's Certificate issued under the authority of the Education Law, or a diploma from a state normal school or the state normal college, and certainly, if they have been appointed and received a Certificate of Appointment from the Board of Higher Education, they have been appointed and hold a Teacher's Certificate under the authority of the Education Law. It does not seem logical that the section was ever intended to cover a case similar to the case of Bertrand Russell who has been in this country for some time and who has never made any application for citizenship and who apparently, as shall hereafter appear, would be denied citizenship. The section applies generally to "teachers and pupils" and is not limited to elementary and secondary schools, and the court therefore holds that Bertrand Russell is not qualified to teach by reason of the provisions of this section, but the decision herein made is not based solely upon this ground.

The second contention of the petitioner is that no examination of any kind was given to Bertrand Russell at the time of his appointment, and this is borne out by the minutes of the Administrative Committee of the City College of the City of New York and of the Board of Higher Education at the time of his appointment. The Court of Appeals has held in the case of *Becker v. Eisner* (277 N. Y., 143, at page 151) that "We need not at this time undertake to say how far the Legislature may go in exempting all positions under the Board of Higher Education from competitive examinations. Until it is determined by the Legislature or some other body that such examinations are impracticable, the Constitution (Article V, Section 6) is to be enforced.

"The power of the Legislature in this particular discussed in *Matter of Ottinger v. Civil Service Commission* (240 N. Y., 435), which authority condemns as illegal this attempt to legislate into an exempt class all positions for which there has not been heretofore an examination."

In *Sloat v. Board of Examiners* (274 N. Y., 367, 370) the Court of Appeals stated: "Statutes and administrative orders, alike, must conform to the mandate of the Constitution. They cannot authorize a procedure which would disregard or nullify that mandate. A person aggrieved by an order or determination of an administrative board or officer which has such result may, in proper case, appeal for redress to the courts (*Matter of Barthelmess v. Cukor*, 231 N. Y., 435). Upon such appeal the courts are not to be satisfied by lip-service. Disobedience or evasion of a constitutional mandate may not be tolerated even though such disobedience might, perhaps, at least temporarily, promote in some respects the best interests of the public. Arbitrary decision that in a given case it is not practicable to ascertain merit and fitness by competitive examination may be challenged and is subject to review by the courts (*Matter of Keymer*, 148 N. Y., 219; *Matter of Scahill v. Drzewucki*, 269 N. Y., 343). An examination is not competitive merely because it is so denominated. The substance, not merely the form, of a competitive examination is required."

In *Matter of Carow v. Board of Education* (272 N. Y., 341, 347), the Court of Appeals said: "The Constitution (Article V, Section 6) in part provides that 'appointments and promotions in the civil service of the state, and of all the civil divisions thereof, including cities and villages, shall be made according to merit and fitness to be ascertained, so far as practicable, by examinations, which, *so far as practicable, shall be competitive.*' The Legislature may not disregard, evade, or weaken the force of that mandate. It applies to every position in the civil service of the state, but within limits which we have attempted to define in other

[2 1 6]

cases, the Legislature may determine whether it is practicable to ascertain merit and fitness for a particular position by competitive examination, or, indeed, by any examination.

"Even casual consideration of the offices comprised in the unclassified civil service leaves little doubt that the Legislature in most cases determined that it was not practicable to ascertain merit and fitness by examination, and intended that both in appointment and removal the appointing officers should be free to pass upon the merit and fitness of those appointed by them; and in most cases the legislative determination may hardly be challenged as unreasonable. In the case, however, of teachers in the public schools in large cities, it might well be argued that a determination by the Legislature that appointments and promotions according to merit and fitness ascertained by competitive examination is impracticable would be arbitrary."

While it is not necessary for this court to adjudicate the action of the Board of Higher Education in proceeding by assuming that a competitive examination for the position of Professor of Philosophy in City College was impracticable, such assumption on the part of the Board of Higher Education is held to be unwarranted, arbitrary and capricious and in direct violation of the plain mandate of the Constitution of the State of New York. If there were only one person in the world who knew anything about philosophy and mathematics and that person was Mr. Russell, the taxpayers might be asked to employ him without examination, but it is hard to believe, considering the vast sums of money that have been spent on American education, that there is no one available, even in America, who is a credit both to learning and to public life. Other universities and colleges, both public and private, seem to be able to find American citizens to employ, and to say that the College of the City of New York could not employ a professor of philosophy by an examination of some sort is an assumption by the Board of Higher Education of the power which was denied to them by the people of the State of New York in the Constitution and no Legislature and no board can violate this mandate.

[2 1 7]

The foregoing reasons would be sufficient to sustain the petition and to grant the relief prayed for but there is a third ground on which the petitioner rests and which, to the court, seems most compelling. The petitioner contends that the appointment of Bertrand Russell has violated the public policy of the state and of the nation because of the notorious immoral and salacious teachings of Bertrand Russell and because the petitioner contends he is a man not of good moral character.

It has been argued that the private life and writings of Mr. Russell have nothing whatsoever to do with his appointment as a teacher of philosophy. It has also been argued that he is going to teach mathematics. His appointment, however, is to the department of philosophy in City College.

In this consideration I am completely dismissing any question of Mr. Russell's attacks upon religion, but there are certain basic principles upon which this government is founded. If a teacher, who is a person not of good moral character, is appointed by any authority the appointment violates these essential prerequisites. One of the prerequisites of a teacher is good moral character. In fact, this is a prerequisite for appointment in civil service in the city and state, or political subdivisions, or in the United States. It needs no argument here to defend this statement. It need not be found in the Education Law. It is found in the nature of the teaching profession. Teachers are supposed not only to impart instruction in the classroom but by their example to teach the students. The taxpayers of the City of New York spend millions to maintain the colleges of the City of New York. They are not spending that money nor was the money appropriated for the purpose of employing teachers who are not of good moral character. However, there is ample authority in the Education Law to support this contention.

Section 556 in the same general article, Article XX, entitled "Teachers and Pupils," reads as follows: "A school commissioner shall examine any charge affecting the moral character of any teacher within his district, first giving such teacher reasonable notice of the charge, and an opportunity to defend himself therefrom; and if he find the charge sustained, he shall annul the teacher's certificate, by whomsoever granted, and declare him unfit to teach; and if the teacher holds a certificate of the commissioner of education, or of a former superintendent of public instruction or a diploma of a state normal school, he shall notify the commissioner of education forthwith of such annulment and declaration."

It has been argued that this section does not apply. Assuming it does not apply to the Board of Higher Education specifically, it is a declaration of the public policy of this state. It is inconceivable that the Board of Higher Education would dare to contend that they had the power to appoint persons of bad moral character as teachers in the colleges of the City of New York. If that is their contention, then this proceeding is properly and timely brought. We do not have to go far to find authority for this contention in the decisions of the courts.

In *Epstein v. Board of Education of the City of New York* (162 Misc., 718, 721), Mr. Justice Shientag said: "The board of examiners has the right to expect of applicants for licenses to teach 'a nice and scrupulous sense of honor which is as unlike mere honesty as the fine Damascus blade is unlike a farming implement.' It has a right to expect from them a strong and delicate sense of moral values."

The contention of the petitioner that Mr. Russell has taught in his books immoral and salacious doctrines is amply sustained by the books conceded to be the writings of Bertrand Russell, which were offered in evidence. It is not necessary to detail here the filth which is contained in the books. It is sufficient to record the following. From *Education and the Modern World,* pages 119 and 120: "I am sure that university life would be better, both intellectually and morally, if most university students had temporary childless marriages. This would afford a solution of the sexual urge neither restless nor surreptitious, neither mercenary nor casual, and of such a nature that it need not take up time which ought to be given to work." From *Marriage and Morals,* pages 165 and 166: "For my part, while I am quite con-

[2 1 9]

vinced that companionate marriage would be a step in the right direction, and would do a great deal of good, I do not think that it goes far enough. I think that all sex-relations which do not involve children should be regarded as a purely private affair, and that if a man and a woman choose to live together without having children, that should be no one's business but their own. I should not hold it desirable that either a man or a woman should enter upon the serious business of a marriage intended to lead to children without having had previous sexual experience." ("The peculiar importance attached, at the present, to adultery, is quite irrational." From *What I Believe*, page 50.)

The Penal Law of the State of New York is a most important factor in the lives of our people. As citizens and residents of our city we come within its protective scope. In dealing with human behavior the provisions of the Penal Law and such conduct as therein condemned must not be lightly treated or completely ignored. Even assuming that the Board of Higher Education possesses the maximum power which the Legislature could possibly confer upon it in the appointment of its teachers, it must act so as not to violate the Penal Law or *to encourage the violation of it*. Where it so acts as to sponsor or encourage violations of the Penal Law, and its actions adversely affect the public health, safety, and morals, its acts are void and of no legal effect. A court of equity, with the powers inherent in that court, has ample jurisdiction to protect the taxpayers of the City of New York from such acts as this of the Board of Higher Education.

In *ex rel. Bennett v. Laman* (277 N. Y., 368) the Court of Appeals, in restraining a person without a license from practicing medicine, said, at page 378: "Although invasion of property rights or pecuniary interests is emphasized in some of the earlier cases as a basis for equitable interference, there appeared later a recognition that public health, morals, safety, and welfare of the community equally required protection from irreparable injury." This has been held in other jurisdictions (see *Stead v. Fortner*, 255 Ill., 468, 478; *ex parte Badger*, 226 S. W., 936). The fact that the question may appear to be novel does not even

[2 2 0]

give rise to an inference that a court of equity is without jurisdiction (*Piper v. Hoard,* 107 N. Y., 73, 76).

The Penal Law of the State of New York defines the crime of abduction and provides that a person who uses, or procures to be taken or used, a female under eighteen years of age, when not her husband, for the purpose of sexual intercourse, or a person who entices an unmarried female of any age of previous chaste character to any place for the purpose of sexual intercourse, is guilty of abduction and punishable by imprisonment for not more than ten years (Section 70). Furthermore, the Penal Law provides that even a parent or guardian having legal charge of a female under eighteen years of age and who consents to her being taken by any person for the purpose of sexual intercourse violates the law and is punishable by imprisonment for not more than ten years (Section 70).

As to the crime of rape the Penal Law provides that a person who perpetrates an act of sexual intercourse with a female not his wife under the age of eighteen years, under circumstances not amounting to rape in the first degree, is guilty of rape in the second degree and punishable by imprisonment for not more than ten years (Section 2010).

Section 100 of the Penal Law makes adultery a criminal offense.

Section 2460 of the Penal Law, among other things, provides that any person who shall induce or attempt to induce any female to reside with him for immoral purposes shall be guilty of a felony and on conviction punishable by imprisonment for not less than two years, nor more than twenty years, and by a fine not exceeding $5000.

When we consider the vast amount of money that the taxpayers are assessed each year to enforce these provisions of the law, how repugnant to the common welfare must be any expenditure that seeks to encourage the violation of the provisions of the Penal Law. Conceding *arguendo* that the Board of Higher Education has sole and exclusive power to select the faculty of City College and that its discretion cannot be reviewed or cur-

[2 2 1]

tailed by this court or any other agency, nevertheless such sole and exclusive power may not be used to aid, abet, or encourage any course of conduct tending to a violation of the Penal Law. Assuming that Mr. Russell could teach for two years in City College without promulgating the doctrines which he seems to find necessary to spread on the printed pages at frequent intervals, his appointment violates a perfectly obvious canon of pedagogy, namely, that the personality of the teacher has more to do with forming a student's opinion than many syllogisms. A person we despise and who is lacking in ability cannot argue us into imitating him. A person whom we like and who is of outstanding ability does not have to try. It is contended that Bertrand Russell is extraordinary. That makes him the more dangerous. The philosophy of Mr. Russell and his conduct in the past is in direct conflict and in violation of the Penal Law of the State of New York. When we consider how susceptible the human mind is to the ideas and philosophy of teaching professors, it is apparent that the Board of Higher Education either disregarded the probable consequences of their acts or were more concerned with advocating a cause that appeared to them to present a challenge to so-called "academic freedom" without according suitable consideration of the other aspects of the problem before them. While this court would not interfere with any action of the board in so far as a pure question of "valid" academic freedom is concerned, it will not tolerate academic freedom being used as a cloak to promote the popularization in the minds of adolescents of acts forbidden by the Penal Law. This appointment affects the public health, safety, and morals of the community and it is the duty of the court to act. Academic freedom does not mean academic license. It is the freedom to do good and not to teach evil. Academic freedom cannot authorize a teacher to teach that murder or treason are good. Nor can it permit a teacher to teach directly or indirectly that sexual intercourse between students, where the female is under the age of eighteen years, is proper. This court can take judicial notice of the fact that students in the colleges of the City of New York are under the age of eighteen years, although some of them may be older.

Academic freedom cannot teach that abduction is lawful nor that adultery is attractive and good for the community. There are norms and criteria of truth which have been recognized by the founding fathers. We find a recognition of them in the opening words of the Declaration of Independence, where they refer to the laws of Nature and of Nature's God. The doctrines therein set forth, which have been held sacred by all Americans from that day to this, preserved by the Constitution of the United States and of the several states and defended by the blood of its citizens, recognizing the inalienable rights with which men are endowed by their Creator must be preserved, and a man whose life and teachings run counter to these doctrines, who teaches and practices immorality and who encourages and avows violations of the Penal Law of the State of New York, is not fit to teach in any of the schools of this land. The judicial branch of our government, under our democratic institutions, has not been so emasculated by the opponents of our institutions to an extent to render it impotent to act to protect the rights of the people. Where public health, safety, and morals are so directly involved, no board, administrative or otherwise, may act in a dictatorial capacity, shielding their actions behind a claim of complete and absolute immunity from judicial review. The Board of Higher Education of the City of New York has deliberately and completely disregarded the essential principles upon which the selection of any teacher must rest. The contention that Mr. Russell will teach mathematics and not his philosophy does not in any way detract from the fact that his very presence as a teacher will cause the students to look up to him, seek to know more about him, and the more he is able to charm them and impress them with his personal presence, the more potent will grow his influence in all spheres of their lives, causing the students in many instances to strive to emulate him in every respect.

In considering the power of this court to review the determination and appointment of Dr. Russell by the Board of Higher Education this court has divided the exhibits in this proceeding into two classes, namely, those exhibits which dealt with controversial measures not *malum in se* as far as the law is concerned, even though abhorrently repulsive to many people, and those considered *malum in se* by the court. Dr. Russell's views on masturbation such as expressed in his book entitled *Education and the Good Life,* at page 211, in which he goes on to state: "Left to itself, infantile masturbation has, apparently, no bad effect upon health, and no discoverable bad effect upon character; the bad effects which have been observed in both respects are it seems wholly attributable to attempts to stop it. . . . Therefore, difficult as it may be, the child should be let alone in this respect"; his views on nudity as expressed in the same book, on page 212, in which he goes on to state: "A child should, from the first, be allowed to see his parents and brothers and sisters without their clothes whenever it so happens naturally. No fuss should be made either way; he should simply not know that people have feelings about nudity"; his views on religion and politics; his own personal life and conduct, with the incidental convictions and libels, are all matters that this court holds to be proper subjects to be considered by the Board of Higher Education in appraising the moral character of Dr. Russell as a professor, and on these subjects the determination of the Board of Higher Education is final. If the standards of the Board of Higher Education in these respects are lower than common decency requires, the remedy is with the appointing power who may be held responsible for appointing individuals with moral standards below that required for the public good. But as to such conduct this court is powerless to act because of the power conferred by law on the Board of Higher Education. But where the matter transcends the field of controversial issues and enters the field of criminal law then this court has the power and is under a duty to act. While in encouraging adultery in the language used in the book *Education and the Good Life,* at page 221, "I shall not teach that faithfulness to our partner through life is in any way desirable, or

[2 2 4]

that a permanent marriage should be regarded as excluding temporary episodes," it might be urged that he is only encouraging the commission of a misdemeanor rather than a felony, yet that mitigating argument must fall when we are confronted with Dr. Russell's utterances as to the damnable felony of homosexualism, which warrants imprisonment for not more than twenty years in New York State, and concerning which degenerate practice Dr. Russell has this to say in his book entitled *Education and the Modern World*, at page 119: "It is possible that homosexual relations with other boys would not be very harmful if they were tolerated, but even then there is danger lest they should interfere with the growth of normal sexual life later on."

Considering Dr. Russell's principles, with reference to the Penal Law of the State of New York, it appears that not only would the morals of the students be undermined, but his doctrines would tend to bring them, and in some cases their parents and guardians, in conflict with the Penal Law, and accordingly this court intervenes.

The appointment of Dr. Russell is an insult to the people of the City of New York and to the thousands of teachers who were obligated upon their appointment to establish good moral character and to maintain it in order to keep their positions. Considering the instances in which immorality alone has been held to be sufficient basis for removal of a teacher and mindful of the aphorism, "As a man thinketh in his heart, so is he," the court holds that the act of the Board of Higher Education of the City of New York in appointing Dr. Russell to the Department of Philosophy of the City College of the City of New York, to be paid by public funds, is in effect establishing a chair of indecency and in doing so has acted arbitrarily, capriciously, and in direct violation of the public health, safety, and morals of the people and of the petitioner's rights herein, and the petitioner is entitled to an order revoking the appointment of the said Bertrand Russel and discharging him from his said position, and denying to him the rights and privileges and the powers appertaining to his appointment. Settle final order accordingly.

[225]

APPENDIX II

Statement of Committee
on Cultural Freedom

The hue and cry which has recently been raised in some quarters over the appointment of Bertrand Russell, one of the most illustrious of contemporary philosophers, to a chair in philosophy at the College of the City of New York carries with it a serious attack on hard-won principles of academic and cultural freedom. The ultimate implications of the organized campaign against Mr. Russell's appointment menace the integrity of our intellectual life, which consists in the free and open consideration of alternatives honestly held and scientifically reasoned.

The objections that have been advanced against Bertrand Russell will not survive analysis for a moment. They are drawn from the traditional arsenal of abuse and intolerance which enemies of freedom have employed against the inquiring mind since the days of antiquity. Socrates, father of the critical tradition in European philosophy, was charged with "corrupting the morals of youth"; the writings of Thomas Aquinas were proscribed, not many years after his death, as "heretical"; Spinoza, whose *amor dei intellectualis* is but another name for a way of life based upon devotion to objective truth, was denounced as an "atheist."

The history of science and art is replete with cases of persecution of social, political, religious, and philosophical dissenters by men of established power and institutional position who have identified their personal prejudices with unalterable first principles. Our time, as the assault on Mr. Russell indicates, shows no improvement on that earlier condition.

Independently of whether his doctrines are regarded as valid or not, Mr. Bertrand Russell is acknowledged, by all who are competent to form a judgment, to have won a place in the history of logical and philosophical thought. To receive instruction from a man of his intellectual caliber is a rare privilege for students anywhere. The views our local inquisitors object to have been no obstruction to Mr. Russell's service as a teacher in the Universities of Cambridge, Oxford, Harvard, and Chicago.

To censor Mr. Russell's intellectual activity because some of his views on matters not germane to his chief theoretical interest are objectionable to some members of the community clearly contravenes the Statement on Academic Freedom and Tenure adopted both by the American Association of University Professors and the Association of American Colleges. Any such attempt, if successful, would establish a dangerous precedent soon to be extended to all fields of scientific inquiry; it would open the way to imposing in the United States the worst features of the totalitarian regimes in German and Russian universities.

Whatever his views on marriage, divorce, and birth control, Mr. Russell has the same right to hold them and defend them as have his opponents theirs. His critics should meet him in the open and fair field of intellectual discussion and scientific analysis. They have no right to silence him by preventing him from teaching. The debate over the mores and rules of conduct regarding which they take issue with him is as old as society. The argument cannot be settled by silencing one side.

The issue involved in this appointment is so fundamental that it cannot be compromised without imperiling the whole structure of intellectual freedom upon which American university life rests.

[2 2 7]